# A-Z SOUTH WEST ENGLAND

| | |
|---|---|
| Key to Map Pages | 2-3 |
| Road Maps | 4-33 |
| Town Plans, Airports & Port Plans | 34-35 |
| Index to Towns and Villages | 36-48 |

## REFERENCE

| | |
|---|---|
| Motorway | **M5** |
| Under Construction | |
| Proposed | |
| Motorway Junctions with Numbers | |
| Unlimited Interchange **4**    Limited Interchange **5** | |
| Motorway Service Area (with fuel station) | **EXETER** Ⓢ |
| with access from one carriageway only | Ⓢ |
| Major Road Service Areas (with fuel station) | **CORNWALL** |
| with 24 hour facilities | Ⓢ |
| Primary Route (with junction number) | **A30** 🔟 |
| Primary Route Destination | **REDRUTH** |
| Dual Carriageways (A & B Roads) | |
| Class A Road | **A30** |
| Class B Road | **B3187** |
| Major Roads Under Construction | |
| Major Roads Proposed | |
| Fuel Station | 🅿 |
| Gradient 1:5(20%) & Steeper (Ascent in direction of arrow) | « |
| Toll | Toll | |
| Mileage between Markers | 8 |
| Railway and Station | |
| Level Crossing and Tunnel | |
| River or Canal | |
| County or Unitary Authority Boundary | |
| National Boundary | |
| Built-up Area | |
| Village or Hamlet | |
| Wooded Area | |
| Spot Height in Feet | • 813 |
| Relief Above 400' (122m) | |
| National Grid Reference (Kilometres) | ¹30 |
| Area Covered by Town Plan | **SEE PAGE 34** |

## TOURIST INFORMATION

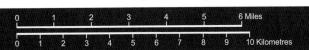

| | |
|---|---|
| | ✈ |
| | ✈ |
| | Ⓗ |
| | 1066 ✈ |
| | 🏰 |
| Castle with Garden (open to public) | Ⓜ |
| Cathedral, Abbey, Church, Friary, Priory | ✝ |
| Country Park | 🏕 |
| Ferry (vehicular) | ⛴ 🚢 |
| (foot only) | ⛟ |
| Garden (open to public) | ✿ |
| Golf Course | 9 Hole 🏌₉    18 Hole 🏌₁₈ |
| Historic Building (open to public) | 🏛 |
| Historic Building with Garden (open to public) | 🏛 |
| Horse Racecourse | 🏇 |
| Lighthouse | 🗼 |
| Motor Racing Circuit | 🏁 |
| Museum, Art Gallery | 🖼 |
| National Park | |
| National Trust Property | (open) NT |
| | (restricted opening) NT |
| Nature Reserve or Bird Sanctuary | 🐦 |
| Nature Trail or Forest Walk | 🍃 |
| Place of Interest | Monument • |
| Picnic Site | 🏕 |
| Railway, Steam or Narrow Gauge | 🚂 |
| Theme Park | 🎡 |
| Tourist Information Centre | 🅸 |
| Viewpoint | (360 degrees) 🔆 |
| | (180 degrees) 🔅 |
| Visitor Information Centre | **V** |
| Wildlife Park | ⚕ |
| Windmill | 🗼 |
| Zoo or Safari Park | 🐘 |

## SCALE

| 0 | 1 | 2 | 3 | 4 | 5 | 6 Miles |
|---|---|---|---|---|---|---|
| 0 1 2 3 4 5 6 7 8 9 10 Kilometres | | | | | | |

Map Pages 4-33
1:158,400
2.5 Miles to 1 Inch

EDITION 1    2023

**2**

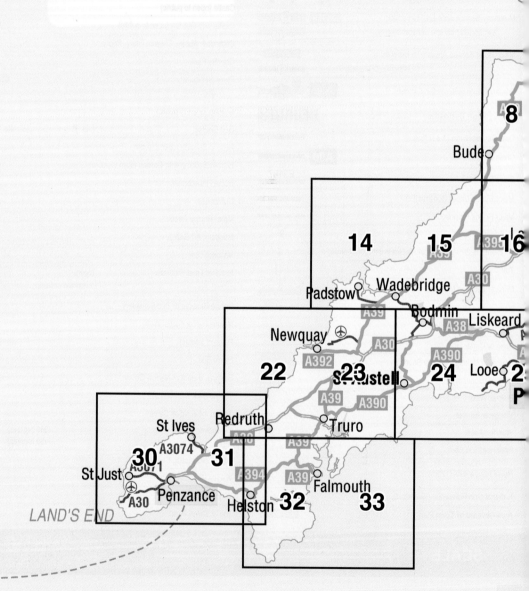

B R I S T O L   C

*LUNDY*

8

Bude

14    15    16

A393

A39

A30

Padstow    Wadebridge

Bodmin    Liskeard

A39    A38

A30

Newquay    A390

22    A392    23 St Austell    24    Looee    2

P

A39    A390

Redruth    A30    Truro

30    A3074    31    A39

St Ives

A30    A394    A39    Falmouth

St Just    Penzance    32    33

A30    Helston

*LAND'S END*

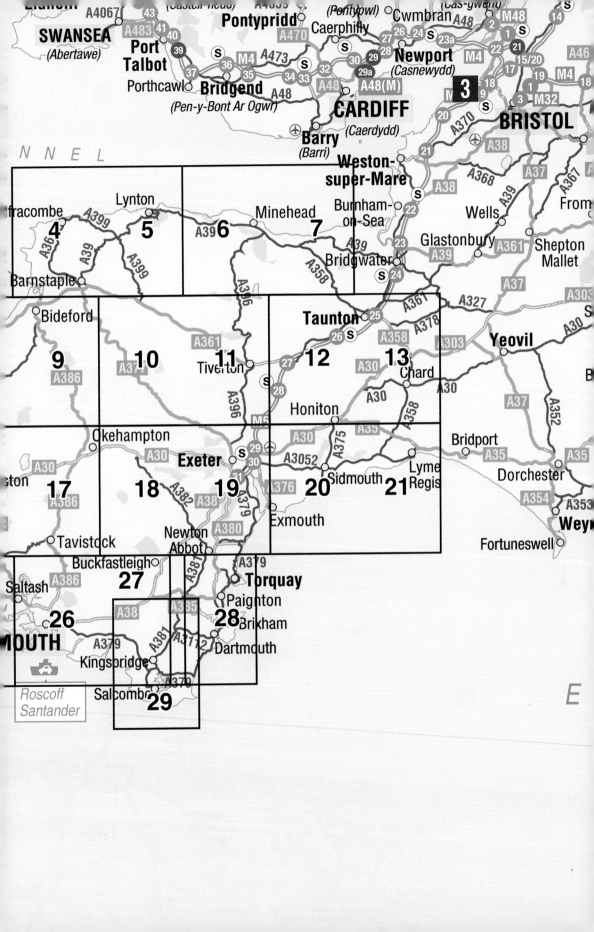

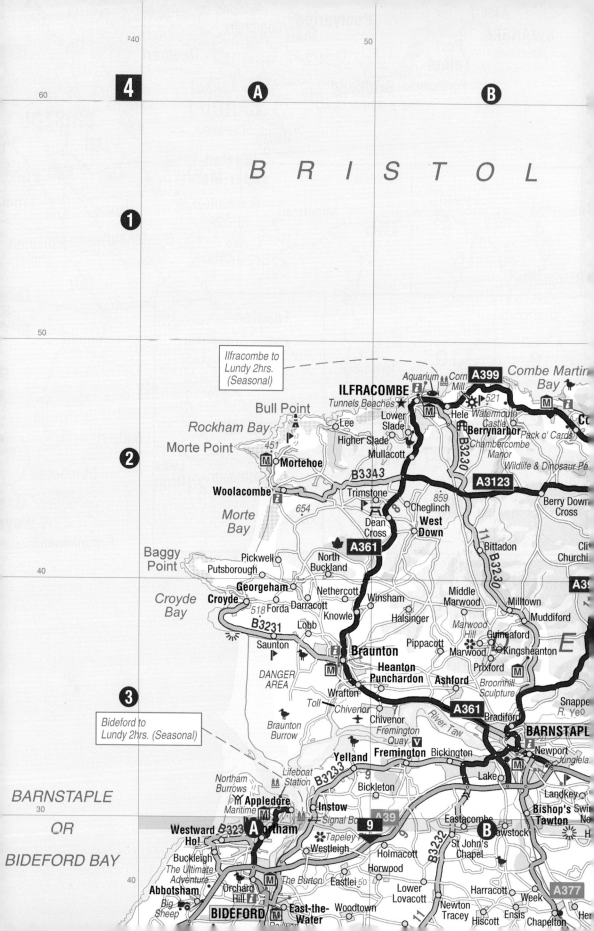

**4**　**Ⓐ**　**Ⓑ**

240　50　60　50

B R I S T O L

**1**

**2**

**3**

*Ilfracombe to Lundy 2hrs. (Seasonal)*

Aquarium　Corn Mill
**A399**　Combe Martin Bay
**ILFRACOMBE**
Tunnels Beaches　Hele　Watermouth Castle
Lower Slade　Berrynarbor　Pack o' Cards
*Bull Point*
*Rockham Bay*　Lee　Higher Slade　Chambercombe Manor
*Morte Point*　Mullacott　Wildlife & Dinosaur Pa
451　B3343　Trimstone　**A3123**
**Mortehoe**　859　Berry Down Cross
**Woolacombe**　Cheglinch
*Morte Bay*　654　Dean Cross　**West Down**
Bittadon　Cli Churchi
*Baggy Point*　Pickwell　**A361**　North Buckland
Putsborough　Nethercott　Middle Marwood　Milltown
**Georgeham**　Winsham　Muddiford
*Croyde Bay*　**Croyde**　Darracott　*Marwood Hill*　Guineaford
518　Forda　Knowle　Halsinger　Marwood　Kingsheanton
**B3231**　Lobb　Pippacott　Prixford
Saunton　*Broomhill Sculpture*
*DANGER AREA*　**Braunton**　**Heanton Puncharden**　Ashford
Wrafton　Snappe R. Yeo
Toll　Chivenor　**A361**　Bradford
*Bideford to Lundy 2hrs. (Seasonal)*
*Braunton Burrow*　Chivenor　**BARNSTAPL**
Fremington Quay　Newport
**Fremington**　Bickington　Jungle la
**Yelland**　Lake
Lifeboat Station　**B3233**　Bickleton　Landkey
*Northam Burrows*　**A39**
**BARNSTAPLE**　**Appledore**　**Instow**　Eastacombe　**Bishop's Tawton**
**OR**　Maritime　Signal Bo　**9**　awstock　Ne
Westward Ho!　**B323**　Ortham　Tapeley　St John's Chapel
**BIDEFORD BAY**　Westleigh　Holmacott　**B3232**　**Ⓑ**
Buckleigh　Horwood
The Ultimate Adventure　The Burton　Eastlei　50　Lower Lovacott　Harracott　Week　**A377**
Abbotsham　Orchard Hill　Woodtown　Newton Tracey　Ensis　Chapelton
Big Sheep
**BIDEFORD**　**East-the-Water**　Hiscott　Her

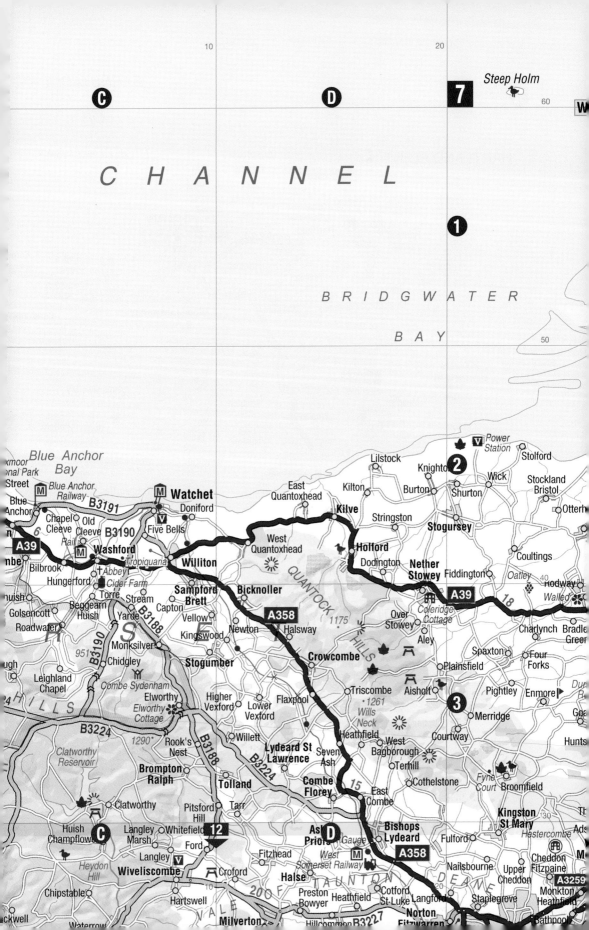

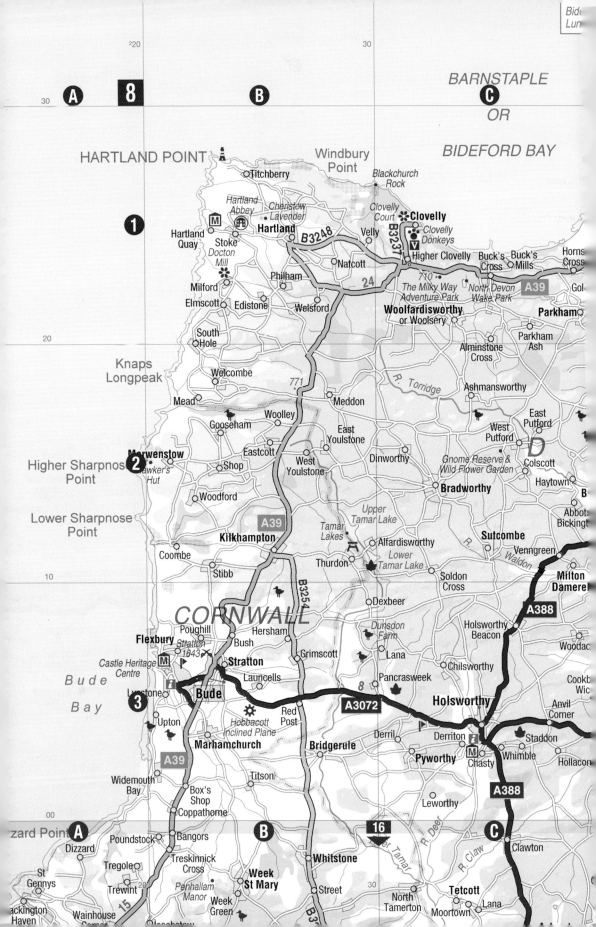

²20    30

30

BARNSTAPLE

OR

BIDEFORD BAY

HARTLAND POINT    Windbury
Point

**1**

•Titchberry    Blackchurch
Rock

Hartland
Abbey    Cheristow
Lavender    Clovelly
Court    ✿Clovelly
Hartland    **HARTLAND**    Velly    Clovelly
Quay    Stoke    B3248    Donkeys
Docton    Ⓜ    ♠    V    Higher Clovelly
Mill    Buck's    Buck's    Horns
710•    Cross    Mills    Cross
Natcott    The Milky Way    North Devon    A39
Philham    24    Adventure Park    Wake Park    Gol
Milford    Welsford    Woolfardisworthy    Parkham
Elmscott    •Edistone    or Woolsery    Parkham
Ash
South    Almanstone    Ash
Hole    Cross

20

Knaps    Welcombe    R. Torridge    Ashmansworthy
Longpeak    771    Meddon
Mead•    Woolley    East    West    East
Gooseham    Youlstone    Putford    Putford
**2**    Eastcott    West    Dinworthy    Gnome Reserve &    Colscott
Higher Sharpnose    Hawker's    Shop    Youlstone    Wild Flower Garden    Haytown
Point    Hut    Woodford    **Bradworthy**    B

Lower Sharpnose    Upper    Abbots
Point    Tamar Lake    Bickingt
**A39**    Tamar    Sutcombe
**Kilkhampton**    Lakes    Alfardisworthy    Venngreen
Coombe    Thurdon    Lower    Soldon    Milton
Tamar Lake    Cross    Damerel
Stibb    Dexbeer    A388

10    Dunsdon    Holsworthy    Woodac
**CORNWALL**    Farm    Beacon
Poughill    Hersham    Lana    Chilsworthy    Cookb
**Flexbury**    Bush    Grimscott    Pancrasweek    Wic
Castle Heritage    Stratton    8    **Holsworthy**    Anvil
Centre    1643    **Stratton**    Corner
*Bude*    Ⓜ    Launcells    Derril    Derriton    Staddon
Lynstone    i    **Bude**    A3072    Ⓜ    Whimble    Hollacon
**3**    Upton    Red    **Bridgerule**    **Pyworthy**    Chasty
*Bay*    Hobbacott    Post    Leworthy    A388
Inclined Plane    **Marhamchurch**
A39    Titson
Widemouth    Box's
Bay    Shop
Coppathorne
00    **A**    **B**    16    **C**
zard Point    Bangors    Clawton
Dizzard    Poundstock    Treskinnick    **Whitstone**
Tregole    Cross    Street    **Tetcott**
St    Trewint    Penhallam    **Week**    North    Moortown    Lana
Gennys    Manor    **St Mary**    Tamerton
ackington    15    Week
Haven    Wainhouse    Green    B3

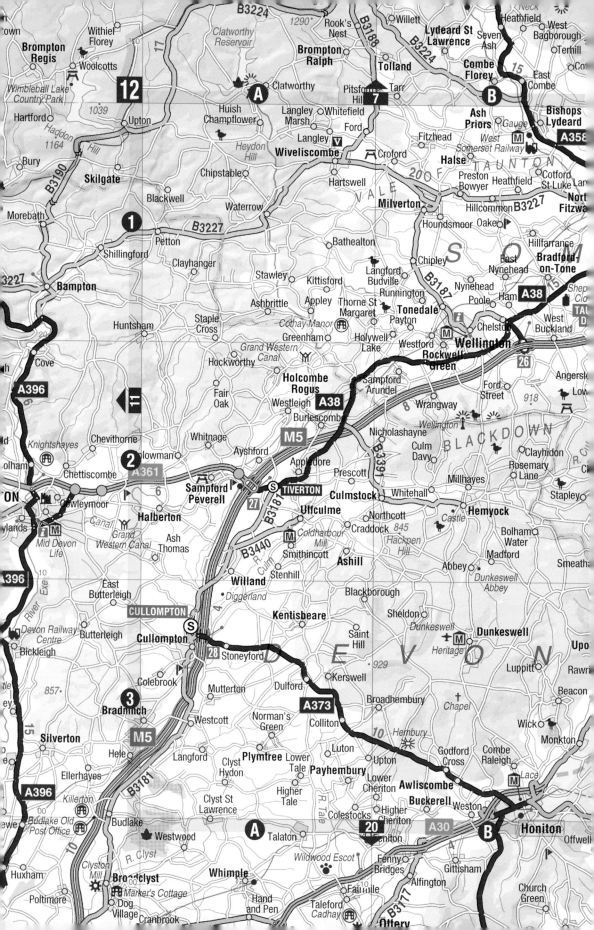

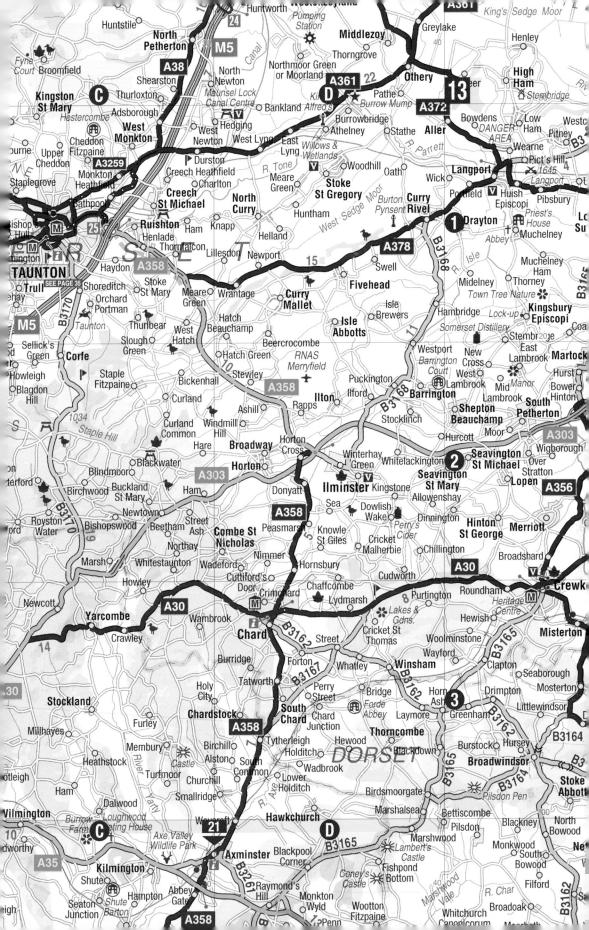

*C E L T I C*

*S E A*

TREVOSE HEAD

*Quies*

*Constantine Bay*

Harlyn Bay

Constantine Bay

Treyarnon

Porthcothan

Park Head

*Berryl's Point*

Mawgan Porth

Trevarrian

**Trenance**

*Japanese*

St Mawgan

*Bedruthan Steps*

Treburrick

St Ervan

St Eval

Rumford

Tredinnick

St Jidgey

*Cornish Birds of Prey Centre*

Talskiddy

Winnard's Perch

*Camel Creek*

*St Breock Downs*

683

*Nine Maidens Stone Row*

*Monolith*

Rosenannon

**Newland**

Rumps Point

*The Mouls*

Pentire Point

*Cliff Castle*

New Polzeath

Port Quin Bay

Port Quin

*Lifebo Stati*

*Padstow Bay*

Polzeath

*Porleath Bee Centre*

*Long Cross Victorian*

**Trelights**

B331

Gunver Head

**Trebetherick**

Trevanger

Pityme

*Lifeboat Station*

**St Minver**

Crugmeer

*Prideaux Place*

**Trevone**

**Rock**

Lowe Ambl

*Lifeboat Station*

Stoptide

*National Lobster Hatchery*

**Padstow**

B3276

Treator

St Merryn

Shop

Little Petherick

Trevance

Edmonton

Whitecross

Trevanson

Eglos

St Issey

Trenance

7

*Royal Cornwall Showground*

St Breock

*Mellingey*

*Mill*

Penrose

Pawton Quoit

A389

14

Old MacDonald's Farm

*Rosenannon*

Rumps Point

Pawton Quoit

B3274

Withi

Ru

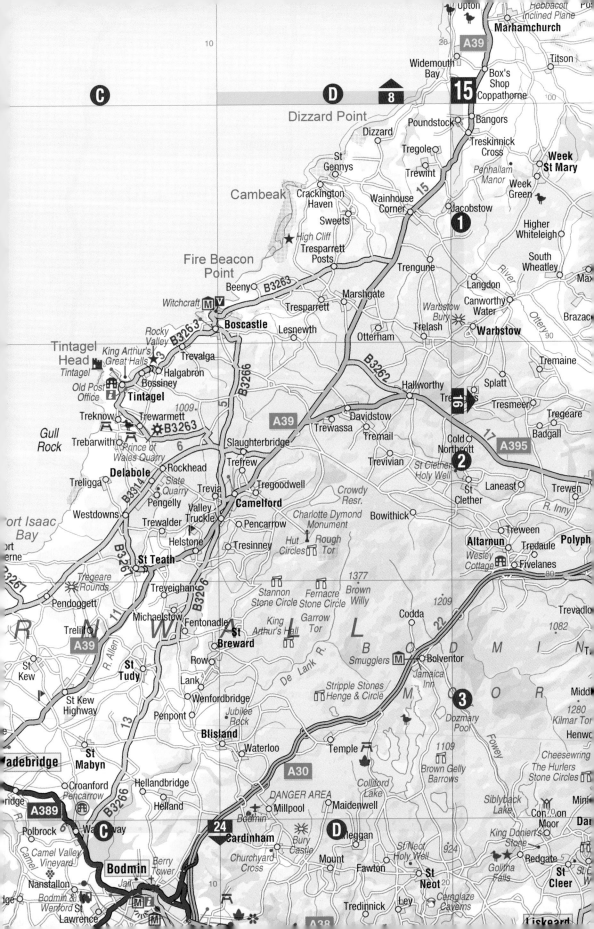

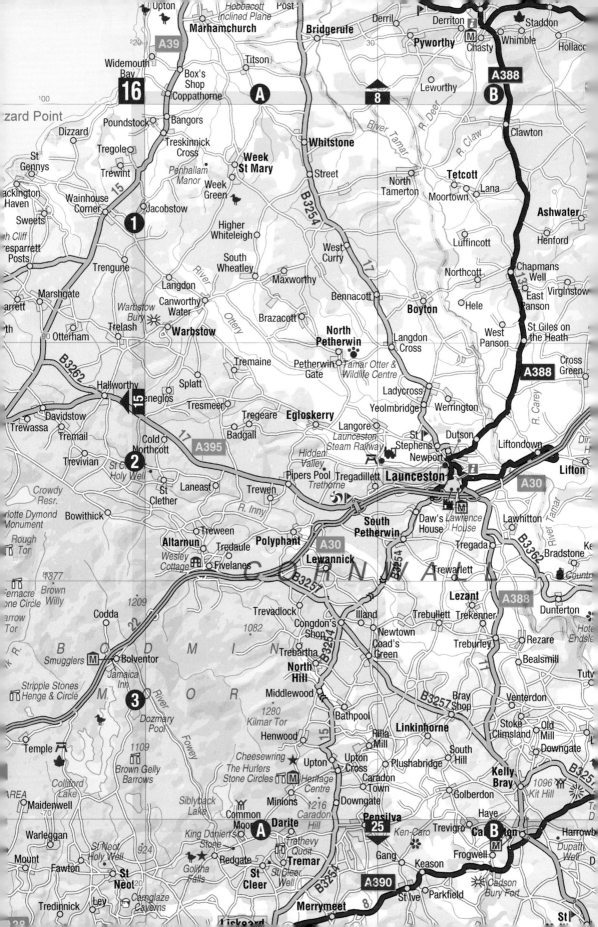

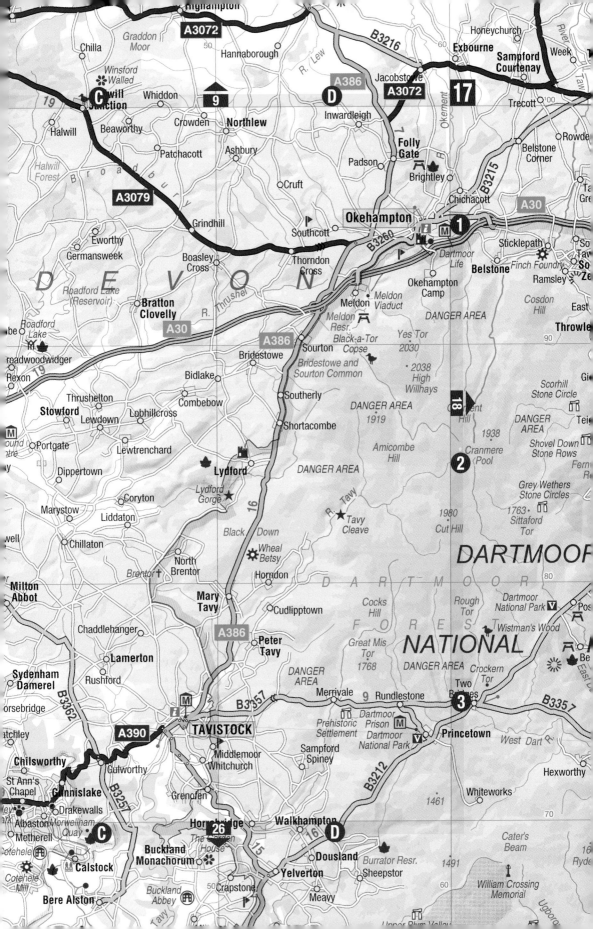

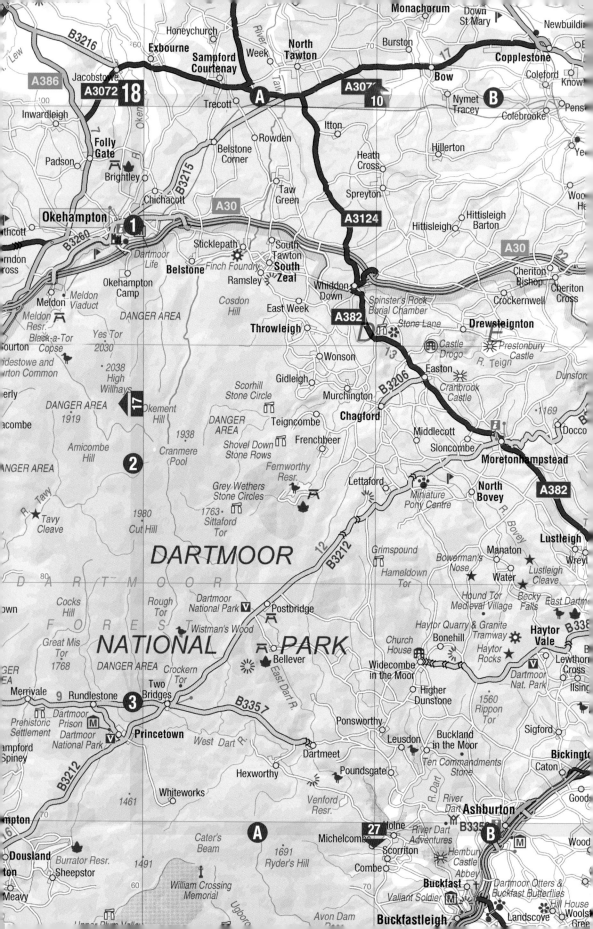

# Map content

**Silverton** · Westcott · Colliton · Hembury · Wick · Monkton

M5 · Langford · Clyst Hydon · **Plymtree** · Lower Tale · **Payhembury** · Luton · Upton · Godford Cross · Combe Raleigh · Lace

Hele · **A396** · Ellerhayes · Clyst St Lawrence · Higher Tale · Lower Cheriton · **Awliscombe** · **Buckerell** · Weston · **B**

**20** · Killerton · Budlake · **A** · Talaton · Colestoc · Higher Cheriton · **A30** · **Honiton** · Offv

Budlake Old Post Office · Westwood · Feniton · **12**

Rewe · **R. Clyst** · Wildwood Escot · Fenny Bridges · Gittisham · Church Green

Huxham · Clyston Mill · **Broadclyst** · **Whimple** · Fairmile · Alfington · **B3177**

Poltimore · Marker's Cottage · Hand and Pen · Taleford Cadhay · **Ottery St Mary** · Farway · W

Pinhoe · Dog Village · Cranbrook · Rockbeare · **B3174** · **B3174** · Tumbling Weir · **A375** · Broad Down

Whipton · Clyst Honiton · **EXETER** · Allercombe · West Hill · Fluxton · Wiggaton · Ark Pottery · Sand

eavitree · **29** · Sowton · Marsh Green · Broad Oak · Metcombe · Coombe · **Sidbury** · Harcombe

**S** · **EXETER** · **Clyst St Mary** · Farringdon · **B3184** · Aylesbeare · **B3180** · Venn Ottery · Tipton St John · Bowd · **Sidford**

**A3015** · **30** · Westpoint Exeter · **A3052** · Southerton · Harpford · **A375** · The Donkey Sanctuary

**M5** · Creaty · Burrow · **Newton Poppleford** · Sid · Weston · **Bransco**

Lower Wear · **Topsham** · Clyst St George · Woodbury Salterton · **B3180** · **B3178** · Salcombe Regis

**B3179** · **Woodbury** · Hawkerland · **B3116** · **SIDMOUTH**

Topsham · Ebf · **DANGER AREA** · Stowford · **Colaton Raleigh**

**A379** · Exton · Woodbury Castle · Bicton Park Botanical

Powderham · Woodmanton · Yettington · **Otterton**

**2** · **A376** · A la Ronde · Chapel · Mill

Kenton · Lympstone · Bystock · **East Budleigh**

South Town · **Starcross** · Hulham · Knowle · Kersbrook

**B3179** · Withycombe Raleigh · Fairlynch

**Cockwood** · **A379** · **EXMOUTH** · Littleham · **Budleigh Salterton**

World of Country Life · Lifeboat Station

**Dawlish Warren**

**Dawlish** · **3**

Holcombe

**Teignmouth**

Teign Heritage Centre · Shaldon

**E N G L I S H**

70

**Babbacombe** · 00 · 10

Bay

**A** · **B**

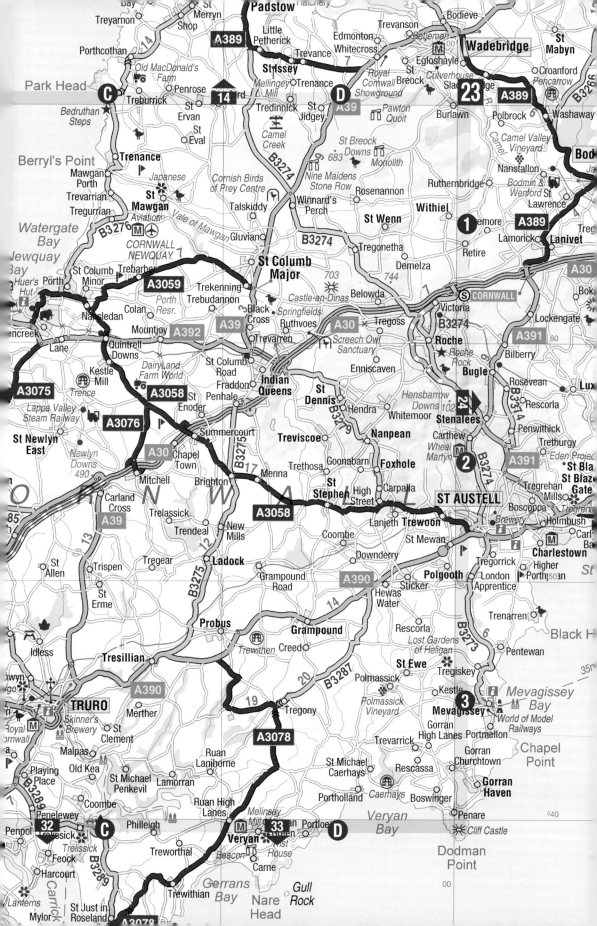

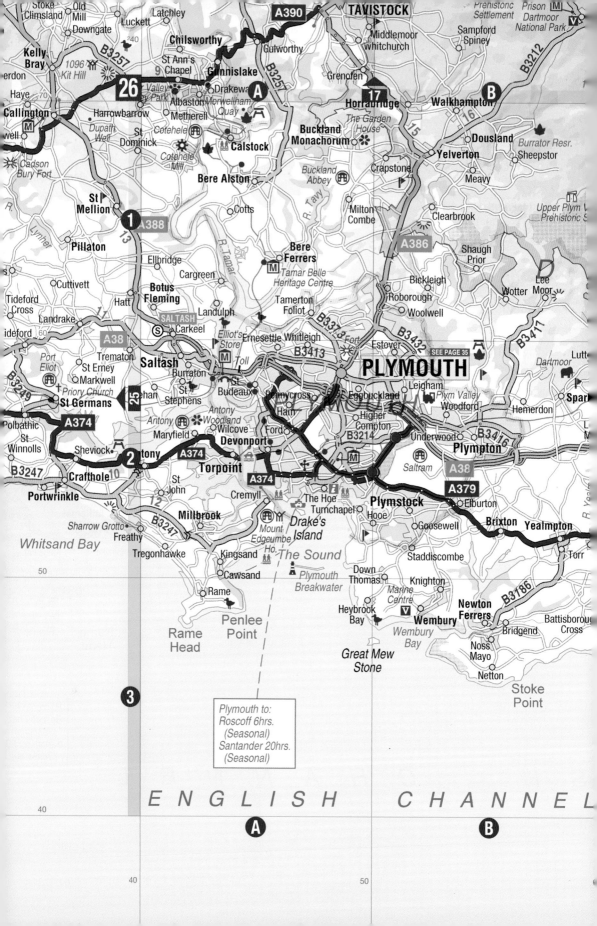

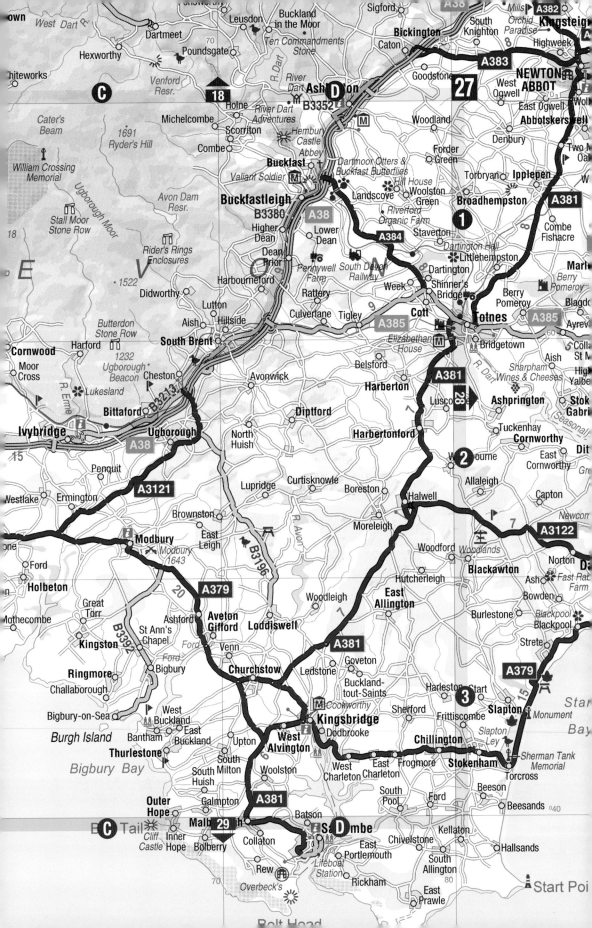

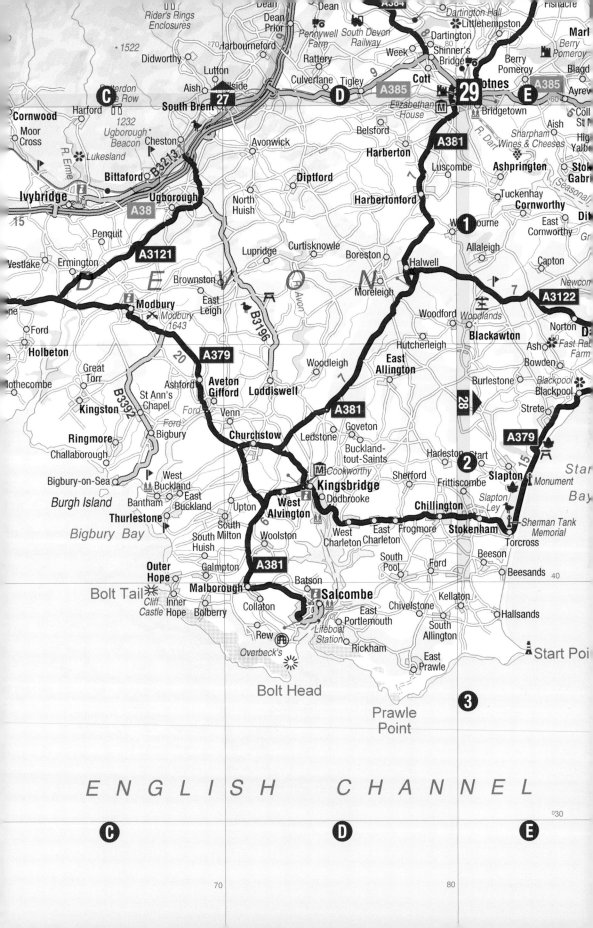

**A** **B**

C E L T I C

**1**

S E A

**40**

The
Carracks

Gurnard's
Head
Zennor
Towednack
Carn Galver Treen
Engine House Porthmeor
Zennor
Quoit
Cripplese

Pendeen
Watch
Morvah
Higher
Bojewyan
•828
9 Maidens
Stone
Circle
Mulfra
Quoit
Nancledr

Levant Mine &
Beam Engine
Men-an-Tol
Chysauster
Ancient Village

**2**
Geevor
Tin Mine
**M** Pendeen
Quoit
Chûn
Castle
Ding Dong
Engine House
New
Mill

Trewellard
Carnyorth
Great
Bosullow
Lanyon
Quoit
Boswarthen

Botallack
Count House **V**
Botallack
Boswens
Standing Stone
Holy Well
**R**

Cape Cornwall
Tregeseal
**8**
Madron
Trevarrack
Gul

The
Brisons
Ballowall
Barrow
St Just
**A3071**
Newbridge
Trengwainton
Heamoor
Chyand

Kelynack
Drift Treneife
**A30**
**M**

**30**
**B3306**
736
Carn Euny
Ancient
Village
Sancreed
Trewidden
Trewidden
Drift
**M** PENZANC

LAND'S END
Brane
Crows-an-wra
**10**
Drift
Newlyn

Whitesand
Bay
Escalls
Kerris
Paul

Lifeboat
Station
**A30**
Boscawen-un
Stone Circle
**B3283**
Pipers
Standing
Stones
Mousehole

Longships
Sennen
Cove
Maen Castle
Sennen
**B3315**
Bird
Hospital
St Cleme
Isle

**3**
Land's
End
Trevescan
St Buryan
Trewoofe

Trevilley
Lamorna

LAND'S END
Telegraph
**M**
Tregiffian
Burial Chamber
Merry Maidens
Stone Circle

Porthcurno
Treen
Penberth
Cribba Head

Porthgwarra
St
Levan
Minack
Theatre
Logan
Rock

Gwennap
Head

Penzance to
Hugh Town 2hrs. 40mins.
(Seasonal)

**20**

**A** Runnel
Stone **B**

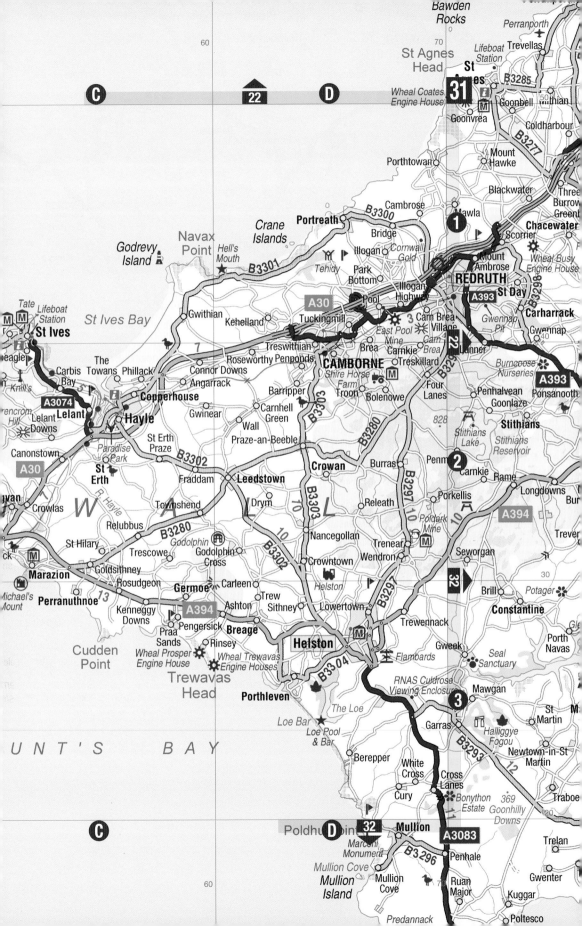

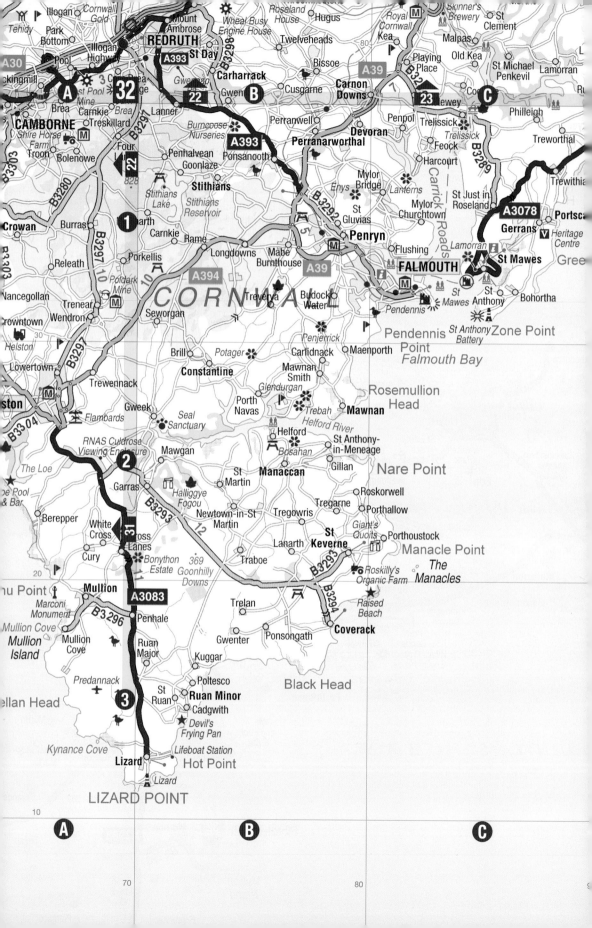

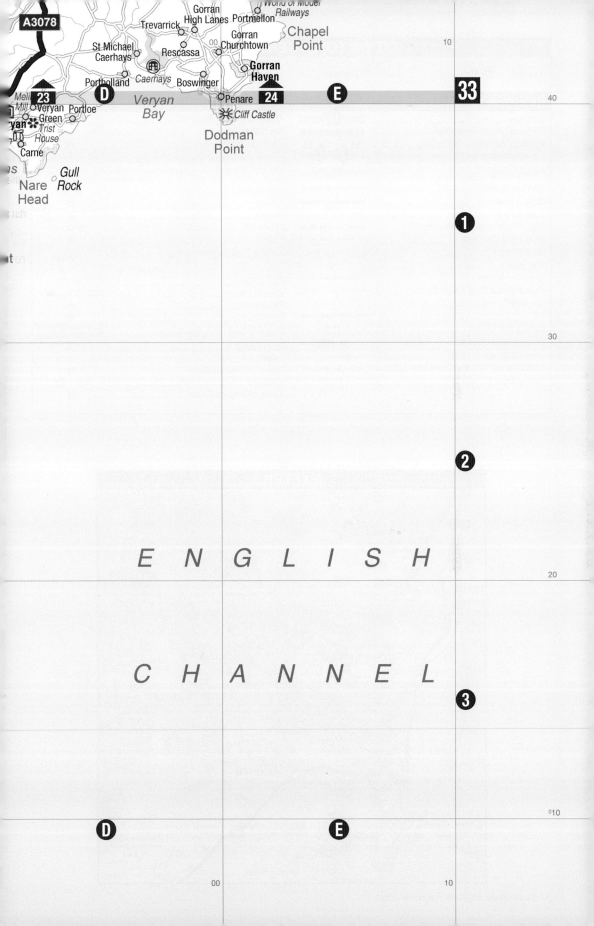

Gorran
High Lanes   Portmellon
Trevarrick                          World of Model
                                    Railways
Gorran              Chapel
St Michael          Churchtown      Point
Caerhays    Rescassa
Portholland   Caerhays   Boswinger   **Gorran
                                     Haven**

Meli
Mill   Veryan   Portloe    Veryan Bay        Penare   **24**
   Green
yan   Trist
      House                            Cliff Castle
Carne                              Dodman
                                   Point

Nare   Gull
Head   Rock

1

2

E   N   G   L   I   S   H
                                                          20

C   H   A   N   N   E   L
                                    3

                                                          °10

**D**                    **E**

00                       10

## Reference to Town Plans

| | | | |
|---|---|---|---|
| Motorway | M5 | Abbey, Cathedral, Priory etc. | ✝ |
| Motorway Under Construction | | Bus Station | ⬤ |
| Motorway Junctions with Numbers | 4 ⬤ ⬤ 5 | Car Park (Selection of) | P |
| Unlimited Interchange 4  Limited Interchange 5 | | Church | ✝ |
| | | City Wall | ⏛⏛⏛⏛ |
| Primary Route | A377 | Ferry (vehicular) 🚢 (foot only) ⛴ | |
| Dual Carriageways | A374 | Golf Course | 🏌 🏴 |
| Class A Road | B3212 | Heliport | Ⓗ |
| Class B Road | | Hospital | Ⓗ |
| Major Roads Under Construction | | Lighthouse | 🗼 |
| Major Roads Proposed | | Market | 🏛 |
| Minor Roads | | National Trust Property (open) | NT |
| Fuel Station | ⛽ | (restricted opening) | NT |
| Restricted Access | | Park & Ride | P+ |
| Pedestrianized Road & Main Footway | | Place of Interest | ■ |
| One Way Streets | → → | Police Station | ▲ |
| Toll | Toll | Post Office | ★ |
| Railway and Station | 🚉 | Shopping Area  (Main street and precinct) | |
| Underground / Metro & D.L.R. Station | ⊖ DLR | Shopmobility | 🅰 |
| Level Crossing and Tunnel | ✕ | Toilet | ▽ |
| Tram Stop and One Way Tram Stop | ● ● | Tourist Information Centre | 𝒊 |
| Built-up Area | | Viewpoint | ☼ ☼ |
| | | Visitor Information Centre | Ⓥ |

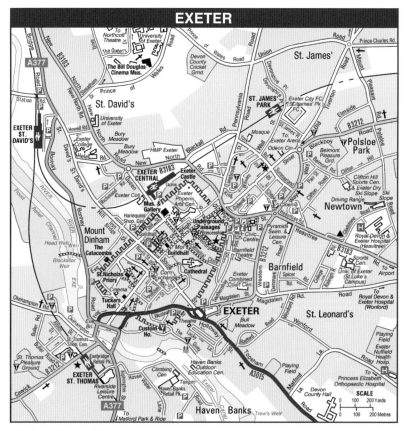

EXETER

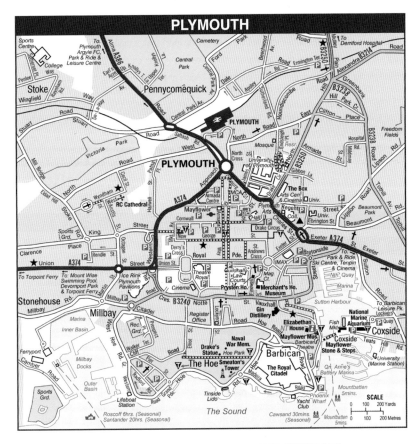

# PLYMOUTH

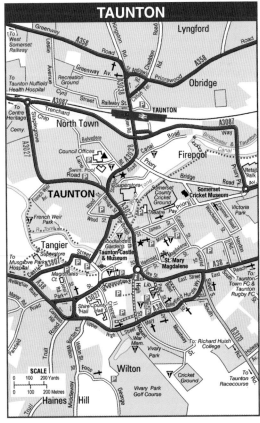

# TAUNTON

1. A strict alphabetical order is used e.g. East Down follows Eastcott but precedes Eastington.

2. The map reference given refers to the actual map square in which the town spot or built-up area is located and not to the place name.

3. Only one reference is given although due to page overlaps the place may appear on more than one page.

4. Where two or more places of the same name occur in the same County or Unitary Authority, the nearest large town is also given; e.g. Aish Devn.....1C 27 (nr Buckfastleigh) indicates that Aish is located in square 1C on page 27 and is situated near Buckfastleigh in the County of Devon.

5. Major towns & destinations are shown in bold i.e. **Exeter** Devn.....**34** (1D **19**). Where they appear on a Town Plan a second page reference is given.

## COUNTIES AND UNITARY AUTHORITIES with the abbreviations used in this index

Cornwall : *Corn*
Devon : *Devn*

Dorset : *Dors*
Plymouth : *Plym*

Somerset : *Som*
Torbay : *Torb*

## INDEX

### A

Abbey Devn ..................................... 2B **12**
Abbey Gate Devn ............................ 1C **21**
Abbots Bickington Devn.................... 2C **8**
Abbotsham Devn............................... 1D **9**
Abbotskerswell Devn ....................... 1A **28**
Accott Devn ...................................... 3C **5**
Adsborough Som ............................. 1C **13**
Aish Devn ........................................ 1C **27**
........................................ (nr Buckfastleigh)
Aish Devn ........................................ 2A **28**
.............................................. (nr Totnes)
Aisholt Som ...................................... 3D **7**
Albaston Corn .................................. 3C **17**
Alcombe Som .................................... 2B **6**
Aley Som .......................................... 3D **7**
Alfardisworthy Devn.......................... 2B **8**
Alfington Devn ................................. 1B **20**
Allaleigh Devn.................................. 2A **28**
Allercombe Devn............................... 1A **20**
Allerford Som.................................... 2B **6**
Allet Corn.......................................... 3B **22**
Allowenshay Som ............................ 2D **13**
Alminstone Cross Devn..................... 1C **8**
Alphington Devn................................ 1D **19**
Alston Devn ...................................... 3D **13**
Alswear Devn.................................... 1B **10**
Altarnun Corn................................... 2A **16**
Alverdiscott Devn.............................. 1E **9**
Alwington Devn................................. 1D **9**
Angarrack Corn................................. 2C **31**
Angersleigh Som............................... 2B **12**
Antony Corn...................................... 2A **26**
Anvil Corner Devn ............................ 3C **8**
Appledore Devn ............................... 3A **4**
.............................................. (nr Bideford)
Appledore Devn ............................... 2A **12**
.............................................. (nr Tiverton)
Appley Som ...................................... 1A **12**
Arlington Devn.................................. 2C **5**
Arlington Beccott Devn...................... 2C **5**
Ash Devn .......................................... 3A **28**
Ashbrittle Som .................................. 1A **12**
Ashburton Devn ............................... 1D **27**
Ashbury Devn ................................... 1D **17**
Ashcombe Devn................................ 3D **19**
Ashford Devn .................................... 3B **4**
.......................................... (nr Barnstaple)

Ashford Devn .................................... 2C **29**
........................................ (nr Kingsbridge)
Ashill Som........................................ 2D **13**
Ashill Devn....................................... 2A **12**
Ashmansworthy Devn ....................... 2C **8**
Ash Mill Devn ................................... 1B **10**
Ashmill Devn..................................... 1B **16**
Ashprington Devn ............................. 2A **28**
Ash Priors Som................................. 1B **12**
Ashreigney Devn............................... 2A **10**
Ash Thomas Devn ............................ 2A **12**
Ashton Corn...................................... 3D **31**
Ashwater Devn.................................. 1B **16**
Athelney Som.................................... 1D **13**
Atherington Devn.............................. 1E **9**
Aveton Gifford Devn.......................... 2C **29**
Avonwick Devn.................................. 2D **27**
Awliscombe Devn.............................. 3B **12**
Axminster Devn................................. 1D **21**
Axmouth Devn .................................. 1C **21**
Aylesbeare Devn............................... 1A **20**
Aylescott Devn.................................. 2A **10**
Ayreville Torb.................................... 1A **28**
Ayshford Devn .................................. 2A **12**

### B

Babbacombe Torb............................. 1B **28**
Badgall Corn..................................... 2A **16**
Bampton Devn................................... 1D **11**
Bangors Corn.................................... 1A **16**
Bankland Som................................... 1D **13**
Bantham Devn................................... 2C **29**
Barbrook Devn.................................. 2D **5**
**Barnstaple** Devn............................. 3B **4**
Barrington Som................................. 2D **13**
Barripper Corn .................................. 2D **31**
Barton Torb....................................... 1B **28**
Barton Town Devn ............................ 2C **5**
Bathealton Som ................................ 1A **12**
Bathpool Corn................................... 3A **16**
Bathpool Som.................................... 1C **13**
Batson Devn...................................... 3D **29**
Battisborough Cross Devn................. 2C **29**
Battleton Som.................................... 1D **11**
Beacon Devn..................................... 3B **12**
Beaford Devn.................................... 2E **9**
Bealsmill Corn................................... 3B **16**
Beaworthy Devn................................ 1C **17**

Beeny Corn....................................... 1D **15**
Beer Devn......................................... 2C **21**
Beercrocombe Som .......................... 1D **13**
Beesands Devn................................. 3A **28**
Beeson Devn..................................... 3A **28**
Beetham Som.................................... 2C **13**
Beggearn Huish Som ........................ 3C **7**
Bellever Devn.................................... 3A **18**
Belowda Corn ................................... 1D **23**
Belsford Devn................................... 2D **27**
Belstone Devn................................... 1A **18**
Belstone Corner Devn ....................... 1A **18**
Bennacott Corn................................. 1A **16**
Bennah Devn..................................... 2C **19**
Bere Alston Devn.............................. 1A **26**
Bere Ferrers Devn............................. 1A **26**
Berepper Corn................................... 3D **31**
Berry Cross Devn.............................. 2D **9**
Berry Down Cross Devn.................... 2B **4**
Berrynarbor Devn.............................. 2B **4**
Berry Pomeroy Devn......................... 1A **28**
Bickenhall Som................................. 2C **13**
Bickington Devn................................ 3B **4**
.......................................... (nr Barnstaple)
Bickington Devn................................ 3B **18**
........................................ (nr Newton Abbot)
Bickleigh Devn.................................. 1B **26**
.............................................. (nr Plymouth)
Bickleigh Devn.................................. 3D **11**
.............................................. (nr Tiverton)
Bickleton Devn.................................. 3B **4**
Bicknoller Som.................................. 3D **7**
**Bideford** Devn................................. 1D **9**
Bidlake Devn..................................... 2D **17**
Bigbury Devn .................................... 2C **29**
Bigbury-on-Sea Devn........................ 2C **29**
Bilberry Corn..................................... 2A **24**
Bilbrook Som .................................... 2C **7**
Birchill Devn ..................................... 3D **13**
Birchwood Som ................................ 2C **13**
Birdsmoorgate Dors.......................... 3D **13**
Bish Mill Devn................................... 1B **10**
Bishop's Hull Som............................. 1C **13**
Bishops Lydeard Som ....................... 1B **12**
Bishop's Nympton Devn.................... 1B **10**
Bishop's Tawton Devn ...................... 3B **4**
Bishopsteignton Devn ...................... 3D **19**
Bishopswood Som ............................ 2C **13**
Bissoe Corn ...................................... 3B **22**

Bittadon *Devn* ............................ 2B **4**
Bittaford *Devn* ........................... 2C **27**
Blackawton *Devn* ...................... 2A **28**
Blackborough *Devn* ................... 3A **12**
Black Cross *Corn* ...................... 1D **23**
Black Dog *Devn* ........................ 3C **11**
Blackdown *Dors* ....................... 3D **13**
Blackmoor Gate *Devn* ............... 2C **5**
Blackpool *Devn* ........................ 3A **28**
Blackpool Corner *Dors* ............. 1D **21**
Black Torrington *Devn* ............... 3D **9**
Blackwater *Som* ........................ 2C **13**
Blackwater *Corn* ....................... 3B **22**
Blackwell *Som* .......................... 1A **12**
Blagdon *Torb* ........................... 1A **28**
Blagdon Hill *Som* ...................... 2C **13**
Blindmoor *Som* ......................... 2C **13**
Blisland *Corn* ........................... 3D **15**
Blue Anchor *Som* ...................... 2C **7**
Blunts *Corn* .............................. 1D **25**
Boasley Cross *Devn* .................. 1D **17**
Bocaddon *Corn* ........................ 2B **24**
Bodieve *Corn* ........................... 3B **14**
Bodinnick *Corn* ........................ 2B **24**
**Bodmin** *Corn* ........................ 1A **24**
Bodmin Airfield *Corn* ................ 3D **15**
Bodrane *Corn* ........................... 1C **25**
Bohortha *Corn* .......................... 1C **32**
Bokiddick *Corn* ......................... 1A **24**
Bolberry *Devn* .......................... 3C **29**
Bolenowe *Corn* ......................... 2D **31**
Bolham *Devn* ........................... 2D **11**
Bolham Water *Devn* ................... 2B **12**
Bolingey *Corn* .......................... 2B **22**
Bolventor *Corn* ......................... 3D **15**
Bondleigh *Devn* ........................ 3A **10**
Bonehill *Devn* .......................... 3B **18**
Boreston *Devn* ......................... 2D **27**
Boscastle *Corn* ........................ 1C **15**
Boscoppa *Corn* ........................ 2A **24**
Bossiney *Corn* .......................... 2C **15**
Bossington *Som* ....................... 2A **6**
Boswarthen *Corn* ...................... 2B **30**
Boswinger *Corn* ........................ 3D **23**
Botallack *Corn* ......................... 2A **30**
Bottreaux Mill *Devn* .................. 1C **11**
Botus Fleming *Corn* .................. 1A **26**
Bovey Tracey *Devn* ................... 3C **19**
Bow *Devn* ................................ 3B **10**
Bowd *Devn* .............................. 2B **20**
Bowden *Devn* ........................... 3A **28**
Bowithick *Corn* ......................... 2D **15**
Box's Shop *Corn* ...................... 3B **8**
Boyton *Corn* ............................. 1B **16**
Bradford *Devn* .......................... 3D **9**
Bradford Barton *Devn* ............... 2C **11**
Bradford-on-Tone *Som* .............. 1B **12**
Bradiford *Devn* ......................... 3B **4**
Bradninch *Devn* ........................ 3A **12**
Bradstone *Devn* ....................... 2B **16**
Bradworthy *Devn* ...................... 2C **8**
Brampford Speke *Devn* ............. 1D **19**
Brandis Corner *Devn* ................. 3D **9**
Brandish Street *Som* ................. 2B **6**
Brane *Corn* .............................. 3B **30**
Branscombe *Devn* .................... 2B **20**
Bratton *Som* ............................ 2B **6**

Bratton Clovelly *Devn* ............... 1C **17**
Bratton Fleming *Devn* ............... 3C **5**
Braunton *Devn* ......................... 3A **4**
Brayford *Devn* .......................... 3C **5**
Bray Shop *Corn* ....................... 3B **16**
Brazacott *Corn* ........................ 1A **16**
Brea *Corn* ............................... 3A **22**
Breage *Corn* ............................ 3D **31**
Brendon *Devn* .......................... 2D **5**
Bridestowe *Devn* ...................... 2D **17**
Bridford *Devn* .......................... 2C **19**
Bridge *Corn* ............................. 3A **22**
Bridge *Som* .............................. 3D **13**
Bridgend *Devn* ......................... 3B **26**
Bridge Reeve *Devn* ................... 2A **10**
Bridgerule *Devn* ....................... 3B **8**
Bridgetown *Som* ....................... 3B **6**
Bridgetown *Devn* ...................... 2A **28**
Brightley *Devn* ......................... 1A **18**
Brighton *Corn* .......................... 2D **23**
Brill *Corn* ................................ 2B **32**
Brimley *Devn* ........................... 3C **19**
**Brixham** *Torb* ....................... 2B **28**
Brixton *Devn* ........................... 2B **26**
Broadclyst *Devn* ....................... 1D **19**
Broadhembury *Devn* ................. 3B **12**
Broadhempston *Devn* ............... 1A **28**
Broad Oak *Devn* ...................... 1A **20**
Broadway *Som* ......................... 2D **13**
Broadwoodkelly *Devn* ............... 3A **10**
Broadwoodwidger *Devn* ............ 2C **17**
Brompton Ralph *Som* ................ 3C **7**
Brompton Regis *Som* ................ 3B **6**
Brownston *Devn* ....................... 2C **27**
Brownstone *Devn* ..................... 3B **10**
Brushford *Som* ......................... 1D **11**
Brushford *Devn* ........................ 3A **10**
Buckerell *Devn* ........................ 3B **12**
Buckfast *Devn* .......................... 1D **27**
Buckfastleigh *Devn* ................... 1D **27**
Buckland Brewer *Devn* .............. 1D **9**
Buckland Filleigh *Devn* .............. 3D **9**
Buckland in the Moor *Devn* ........ 3B **18**
Buckland Monachorum *Devn* ...... 1A **26**
Buckland St Mary *Som* .............. 2C **13**
Buckland-tout-Saints *Devn* ........ 2D **29**
Buckleigh *Devn* ........................ 1D **9**
Buck's Cross *Devn* .................... 1C **8**
Buck's Mills *Devn* ..................... 1C **8**
Bude *Corn* ............................... 3B **8**
Budge's Shop *Corn* ................... 2D **25**
Budlake *Devn* ........................... 3D **11**
Budleigh Salterton *Devn* ........... 2A **20**
Budock Water *Corn* ................... 1B **32**
Bugle *Corn* .............................. 2A **24**
Bulkworthy *Devn* ...................... 2C **8**
Burlawn *Corn* ........................... 1D **23**
Burlescombe *Devn* .................... 2A **12**
Burlestone *Devn* ....................... 3A **28**
Burras *Corn* ............................. 2D **31**
Burraton *Corn* .......................... 2A **26**
Burridge *Som* ........................... 3D **13**
Burrington *Devn* ....................... 2A **10**
Burrow *Devn* ............................ 2A **20**
Burrow *Som* ............................. 2B **6**
Burrowbridge *Som* .................... 1D **13**
Burston *Devn* ........................... 3B **10**

Burton *Som* .............................. 2D **7**
Bury *Som* ................................ 1D **11**
Bush *Corn* ............................... 3B **8**
Butterleigh *Devn* ...................... 3D **11**
Bystock *Devn* ........................... 2A **20**

## C

Cadbury *Devn* .......................... 3D **11**
Cadeleigh *Devn* ........................ 3D **11**
Cadgwith *Corn* ......................... 3B **32**
Callestick *Corn* ........................ 2B **22**
Callington *Corn* ........................ 1D **25**
Calstock *Corn* .......................... 1A **26**
Calverleigh *Devn* ...................... 2D **11**
**Camborne** *Corn* .................... 2D **31**
Cambrose *Corn* ........................ 3A **22**
Camelford *Corn* ........................ 2D **15**
Canonstown *Corn* ..................... 2C **31**
Canworthy Water *Corn* .............. 1A **16**
Capton *Devn* ............................ 2A **28**
Capton *Som* ............................. 3C **7**
Caradon Town *Corn* .................. 3A **16**
Carbis Bay *Corn* ....................... 2C **31**
Cardinham *Corn* ....................... 1B **24**
Cargreen *Corn* ......................... 1A **26**
Carhampton *Som* ..................... 2C **7**
Carharrack *Corn* ...................... 3B **22**
Carkeel *Corn* ........................... 1A **26**
Carland Cross *Corn* .................. 2C **23**
Carleen *Corn* ........................... 3D **31**
Carlidnack *Corn* ....................... 2B **32**
Carlyon Bay *Corn* ..................... 2A **24**
Carn Brea Village *Corn* ............. 3A **22**
Carne *Corn* .............................. 1D **33**
Carnhell Green *Corn* ................. 2D **31**
Carnkie *Corn* ........................... 1B **32**
.................................. (nr Falmouth)
Carnkie *Corn* ........................... 2D **31**
.................................. (nr Redruth)
Carnkief *Corn* .......................... 2B **22**
Carnon Downs *Corn* ................. 3B **22**
Carnyorth *Corn* ........................ 2A **30**
Carpalla *Corn* .......................... 2D **23**
Carthew *Corn* .......................... 2A **24**
Catherston Leweston *Dors* ........ 1D **21**
Caton *Devn* .............................. 3B **18**
Caute *Devn* .............................. 2D **9**
Cawsand *Corn* ......................... 2A **26**
Chacewater *Corn* ..................... 3B **22**
Chaddlehanger *Devn* ................ 3C **17**
Chaffcombe *Som* ..................... 2D **13**
Chagford *Devn* ......................... 2B **18**
Challaborough *Devn* ................. 2C **29**
Challacombe *Devn* ................... 2C **5**
Chapel Amble *Corn* .................. 3B **14**
Chapel Cleeve *Som* .................. 2C **7**
Chapelton *Devn* ....................... 1E **9**
Chapel Town *Corn* .................... 2C **23**
Chapmans Well *Devn* ................ 1B **16**
**Chard** *Som* .......................... 3D **13**
Chard Junction *Dors* ................. 3D **13**
Chardstock *Devn* ...................... 3D **13**
Charles *Devn* ........................... 3C **5**
Charlestown *Corn* ..................... 2A **24**
Charlton *Som* ........................... 1C **13**
Charmouth *Dors* ....................... 1D **21**

Chasty Devn............................ 3C **8**
Chawleigh Devn................................ 2B **10**
Cheddon Fitzpaine Som .................. 1C **13**
Cheglinch Devn................................ 2B **4**
Cheldon Devn .................................. 2B **10**
Chelston Som .................................. 1B **12**
Cheriton Devn .................................. 2D **5**
Cheriton Bishop Devn..................... 1B **18**
Cheriton Cross Devn ...................... 1B **18**
Cheriton Fitzpaine Devn .................. 3C **11**
Cheston Devn .................................. 2C **27**
Chettiscombe Devn.......................... 2D **11**
Chevithorne Devn............................ 2D **11**
Chichacott Devn............................... 1A **18**
Chidgley Som................................... 3C **7**
Chilla Devn ...................................... 3D **9**
Chillaton Devn.................................. 2C **17**
Chillington Devn............................... 2D **29**
Chillington Som................................ 2D **13**
Chilsworthy Corn.............................. 3C **17**
Chilsworthy Devn.............................. 3C **8**
Chilton Devn .................................... 3C **11**
Chipley Som..................................... 1B **12**
Chipstable Som................................ 1A **12**
Chitterley Devn ................................ 3D **11**
Chittlehamholt Devn......................... 1A **10**
Chittlehampton Devn........................ 1A **10**
Chivelstone Devn............................. 3D **29**
Chivenor Devn ................................. 3B **4**
Chivenor Airfield Devn..................... 3A **4**
Christow Devn .................................. 2C **19**
Chudleigh Devn................................ 3C **19**
Chudleigh Knighton Devn................. 3C **19**
Chulmleigh Devn.............................. 2A **10**
Church Green Devn.......................... 1B **20**
Churchill Devn .................................. 3D **13**
.......................................(nr Axminster)
Churchill Devn .................................. 2B **4**
....................................(nr Barnstaple)
Churchinford Som............................ 2C **13**
Churchstanton Som.......................... 2B **12**
Churchstow Devn.............................. 2D **29**
Churchtown Devn ............................ 2C **5**
Churston Ferrers Torb..................... 2B **28**
Chyandour Corn .............................. 2B **30**
Clapham Devn .................................. 2C **19**
Clapworthy Devn.............................. 1A **10**
Clatworthy Som ............................... 3C **7**
Clawton Devn................................... 1B **16**
Clayhanger Devn.............................. 1A **12**
Clayhidon Devn................................ 2B **12**
Clearbrook Devn .............................. 1B **26**
Clifton Devn ..................................... 2C **5**
Clovelly Devn ................................... 1C **8**
Clyst Honiton Devn.......................... 1D **19**
Clyst Hydon Devn............................ 3A **12**
Clyst St George Devn ..................... 2D **19**
Clyst St Lawrence Devn................... 3A **12**
Clyst St Mary Devn ......................... 1D **19**
Coad's Green Corn.......................... 3A **16**
Cobbaton Devn ............................... 1A **10**
Coburg Devn.................................... 3C **19**
Cockington Torb.............................. 1A **28**
Cockwood Devn............................... 2D **19**
Codda Corn...................................... 3D **15**
Coffinswell Devn.............................. 1A **28**
Colan Corn....................................... 1C **23**

Colaton Raleigh Devn...................... 2A **20**
Coldeast Devn.................................. 3C **19**
Coldharbour Corn............................. 3B **22**
Cold Northcott Corn ........................ 2A **16**
Coldridge Devn ............................... 3A **10**
Colebrook Devn................................ 3A **12**
Colebrooke Devn............................. 1B **18**
Coleford Devn .................................. 3B **10**
Colestocks Devn ............................. 3A **12**
Collaton Devn................................... 3D **29**
Collaton St Mary Torb ..................... 1A **28**
Colliton Devn.................................... 3A **12**
Colscott Devn.................................. 2C **8**
Colyford Devn .................................. 1C **21**
Colyton Devn.................................... 1C **21**
Combe Devn..................................... 1D **27**
Combebow Devn.............................. 2C **17**
Combe Fishacre Devn...................... 1A **28**
Combe Florey Som........................... 3D **7**
Combeinteignhead Devn.................. 3D **19**
Combe Martin Devn ......................... 2B **4**
Combe Raleigh Devn....................... 3B **12**
Combe St Nicholas Som .................. 2D **13**
Combpyne Devn.............................. 1C **21**
Common Moor Corn......................... 1C **25**
Compton Devn.................................. 1A **28**
Congdon's Shop Corn ..................... 3A **16**
Connor Downs Corn......................... 2C **31**
Constantine Corn ............................. 2B **32**
Constantine Bay Corn...................... 3A **14**
Cookbury Devn ............................... 3D **9**
Cookbury Wick Devn....................... 3C **8**
Coombe Corn................................... 2B **8**
.............................................. (nr Bude)
Coombe Corn................................... 2D **23**
..........................................(nr St Austell)
Coombe Corn................................... 3C **23**
.............................................. (nr Truro)
Coombe Devn ................................. 1B **20**
..........................................(nr Sidmouth)
Coombe Devn ................................. 3D **19**
.......................................(nr Teignmouth)
Coppathorne Corn............................ 3B **8**
Copperhouse Corn .......................... 2C **31**
Copplestone Devn............................ 3B **10**
Corfe Som........................................ 2C **13**
Cornwall Airport Newquay Corn
.......................................................... 1C **23**
Cornwood Devn ............................... 2C **27**
Cornworthy Devn ............................. 2A **28**
Coryton Devn ................................... 2C **17**
Cotford St Luke Som........................ 1B **12**
Cothelstone Som.............................. 3D **7**
Cotleigh Devn .................................. 3C **13**
Cott Devn......................................... 1D **27**
Cotteylands Devn............................. 2D **11**
Cotts Devn ....................................... 1A **26**
Couch's Mill Corn............................. 2B **24**
Countisbury Devn............................. 2D **5**
Cove Devn ....................................... 2D **11**
Coverack Corn ................................. 3B **32**
Cowley Devn..................................... 1D **19**
Cowleymoor Devn............................ 2D **11**
Crackington Haven Corn .................. 1D **15**
Craddock Devn ................................ 2A **12**
Crafthole Corn.................................. 2D **25**
Cranbrook Devn............................... 1A **20**

Crantock Corn.................................. 1B **22**
Crapstone Devn ............................... 1B **26**
Crawley Devn.................................... 3C **13**
Creacombe Devn.............................. 2C **11**
Crediton Devn .................................. 3C **11**
Creech Heathfield Som .................... 1C **13**
Creech St Michael Som.................... 1C **13**
Creed Corn....................................... 3D **23**
Cremyll Corn..................................... 2A **26**
Cricket Malherbie Som..................... 2D **13**
Cricket St Thomas Som.................... 3D **13**
Crimchard Som................................. 3D **13**
Cripplesease Corn............................ 2C **31**
Croanford Corn ................................ 3C **15**
Crockernwell Devn........................... 1B **18**
Croford Som ..................................... 1B **12**
Cross Green Devn ........................... 2B **16**
Cross Lanes Corn............................. 3D **31**
Cross Side Devn .............................. 1C **11**
Crowan Corn..................................... 2D **31**
Crowcombe Som .............................. 3D **7**
Crowden Devn .................................. 1C **17**
Crowlas Corn.................................... 2C **31**
Crowntown Corn............................... 2D **31**
Crows-an-wra Corn .......................... 3A **30**
Croyde Devn .................................... 3A **4**
Cruft Devn ....................................... 1D **17**
Crugmeer Corn ................................ 3B **14**
Cruwys Morchard Devn.................... 2C **11**
Cubert Corn ..................................... 2B **22**
Cudlipptown Devn............................ 3D **17**
Cudworth Som .................................. 2D **13**
Cullompton Devn ............................. 3A **12**
Culm Davy Devn .............................. 2B **12**
Culmstock Devn............................... 2B **12**
Culver Devn ..................................... 1C **19**
Culverlane Devn............................... 1D **27**
Curland Som .................................... 2C **13**
Curland Common Som...................... 2C **13**
Curry Mallet Som ............................. 1D **13**
Curry Rivel Som ............................... 1D **13**
Curtisknowle Devn............................ 2D **27**
Cury Corn......................................... 3D **31**
Cusgarne Corn................................. 3B **22**
Cutcombe Som ................................ 3B **6**
Cutmadoc Corn................................ 1A **24**
Cuttiford's Door Som........................ 2D **13**
Cuttivett Corn................................... 1D **25**

## D

Dalwood Devn................................... 3C **13**
Darite Corn ...................................... 1C **25**
Darracott Devn................................. 3A **4**
Dartington Devn............................... 1D **27**
Dartmeet Devn................................. 3A **18**
Dartmouth Devn............................... 2A **28**
Davidstow Corn................................ 2D **15**
**Dawlish** Devn............................... 3D **19**
Dawlish Warren Devn....................... 3D **19**
Daw's House Corn ........................... 2B **16**
Dean Devn....................................... 2C **5**
...............................(nr Combe Martin)
Dean Devn....................................... 2D **5**
................................................(nr Lynton)
Dean Cross Devn ............................ 2B **4**
Dean Prior Devn............................... 1D **27**

Delabole *Corn*................................2C **15**
Demelza *Corn*..............................1D **23**
Denbury *Devn*..............................1A **28**
Derril *Devn*.....................................3C **8**
Derriton *Devn*.................................3C **8**
Devonport *Plym*...........................2A **26**
Devoran *Corn*...............................1B **32**
Dexbeer *Devn*................................3B **8**
Didworthy *Devn*............................1C **27**
Dinworthy *Devn*..............................2C **8**
Dippertown *Devn*..........................2C **17**
Diptford *Devn*...............................2D **27**
Dittisham *Devn*.............................2A **28**
Dizzard *Corn*................................1D **15**
Dobwalls *Corn*..............................1C **25**
Doccombe *Devn*...........................2B **18**
Dodbrooke *Devn*..........................2D **29**
Doddiscombsleigh *Devn*...............2C **19**
Dodington *Som*...............................2D **7**
Dog Village *Devn*.........................1D **19**
Dolton *Devn*....................................2E **9**
Doniford *Som*..................................2C **7**
Donyatt *Som*.................................2D **13**
Doublebois *Corn*..........................1B **24**
Dousland *Devn*.............................1B **26**
Dowland *Devn*................................2E **9**
Dowlands *Devn*............................1C **21**
Dowlish Wake *Som*.......................2D **13**
Downderry *Corn*...........................2D **25**
.........................................(nr Looe)
Downderry *Corn*...........................2D **23**
.................................(nr St Austell)
Downgate *Corn*............................3B **16**
...............................(nr Kelly Bray)
Downgate *Corn*............................3A **16**
.............................(nr Upton Cross)
Down St Mary *Devn*......................3B **10**
Down Thomas *Devn*.....................2B **26**
Drakewalls *Corn*...........................3C **17**
Drayford *Devn*..............................2B **10**
Drewsteignton *Devn*.....................1B **18**
Drift *Corn*......................................3B **30**
Drym *Corn*....................................2D **31**
Dulford *Devn*................................3A **12**
Duloe *Corn*...................................2C **25**
Dulverton *Som*.............................1D **11**
Dunchideock *Devn*.......................2C **19**
Dunkeswell *Devn*..........................3B **12**
Dunkeswell Airfield *Devn*..............3B **12**
Dunsford *Devn*.............................2C **19**
Dunster *Som*...................................2B **6**
Dunstone *Devn*............................2B **26**
Dunterton *Devn*............................3B **16**
Durston *Som*................................1C **13**
Dutson *Corn*.................................2B **16**

Eastacombe *Devn*...........................1E **9**
Eastacott *Devn*.............................1A **10**
East Allington *Devn*......................2D **29**
East Anstey *Devn*.........................1C **11**
East Ashley *Devn*.........................2A **10**
East Buckland *Devn*........................3C **5**
..................................(nr Barnstaple)
East Buckland *Devn*.....................2C **29**
...............................(nr Thurlestone)

East Budleigh *Devn*......................2A **20**
East Butterleigh *Devn*..................3D **11**
East Charleton *Devn*....................2D **29**
East Combe *Som*...........................3D **7**
East Cornworthy *Devn*..................2A **28**
Eastcott *Corn*.................................2B **8**
East Down *Devn*.............................2C **5**
Eastington *Devn*...........................3B **10**
East Knowstone *Devn*...................1C **11**
East Leigh *Devn*...........................3A **10**
.........................................(nr Crediton)
East Leigh *Devn*...........................2C **27**
.......................................(nr Modbury)
Eastleigh *Devn*...............................1D **9**
East Looe *Corn*.............................2C **25**
East Lyng *Som*.............................1D **13**
East Nynehead *Som*.....................1B **12**
East Ogwell *Devn*.........................3C **19**
Easton *Devn*.................................2B **18**
East Panson *Devn*........................1B **16**
East Portlemouth *Devn*.................3D **29**
East Prawle *Devn*.........................3D **29**
East Putford *Devn*...........................2C **8**
East Quantoxhead *Som*.................2D **7**
East Stowford *Devn*.....................1A **10**
East Taphouse *Corn*.....................1B **24**
East-the-Water *Devn*......................1D **9**
East Village *Devn*.........................3C **11**
East Week *Devn*...........................1A **18**
East Worlington *Devn*...................2B **10**
East Youlstone *Devn*......................2B **8**
Ebberley Hill *Devn*.........................2E **9**
Ebford *Devn*.................................2D **19**
Edgcott *Som*...................................3A **6**
Edistone *Devn*................................1B **8**
Edmonton *Corn*............................3B **14**
Efford *Devn*..................................3C **11**
Eggbuckland *Plym*.......................2A **26**
Eggesford *Devn*............................2A **10**
Eggesford Airfield *Devn*................3A **10**
Egloshayle *Corn*...........................3C **15**
Egloskerry *Corn*...........................2A **16**
Elburton *Plym*...............................2B **26**
Ellbridge *Corn*..............................1A **26**
Ellerhayes *Devn*...........................3D **11**
Elmscott *Devn*................................1B **8**
Elston *Devn*..................................3B **10**
Elstone *Devn*................................2A **10**
Elworthy *Som*.................................3C **7**
Enniscaven *Corn*..........................2D **23**
Ensis *Devn*.....................................1E **9**
Ermington *Devn*...........................2C **27**
Ernesettle *Plym*............................2A **26**
Escalls *Corn*.................................3A **30**
Estover *Plym*................................2B **26**
Eworthy *Devn*...............................1C **17**
Exbourne *Devn*.............................3A **10**
Exebridge *Som*.............................1D **11**
**Exeter** *Devn*.........................**34 (1D 19)**
Exeter Airport *Devn*
....................................................1A **20**
Exford *Som*.....................................3A **6**
Exminster *Devn*............................2D **19**
**Exmouth** *Devn*.........................2A **20**
Exton *Som*......................................3B **6**
Exton *Devn*...................................2D **19**
Exwick *Devn*.................................1D **19**

Fairmile *Devn*...............................1A **20**
Fair Oak *Devn*..............................2A **12**
Fairy Cross *Devn*............................1D **9**
**Falmouth** *Corn*.........................1C **32**
Farringdon *Devn*...........................1A **20**
Farway *Devn*................................1B **20**
Fawton *Corn*.................................1B **24**
Feniton *Devn*................................1A **20**
Fenny Bridges *Devn*.....................1B **20**
Fentonadle *Corn*...........................3C **15**
Feock *Corn*...................................1C **32**
Filleigh *Devn*................................2B **10**
.........................................(nr Crediton)
Filleigh *Devn*................................1A **10**
.................................(nr South Molton)
Fishpond Bottom *Dors*..................1D **21**
Fitzhead *Som*...............................1B **12**
Five Bells *Som*................................2C **7**
Fivehead *Som*...............................1D **13**
Fivelanes *Corn*.............................2A **16**
Flaxpool *Som*..................................3D **7**
Flexbury *Corn*.................................3B **8**
Flushing *Corn*...............................1C **32**
Fluxton *Devn*................................1A **20**
Folly Cross *Devn*............................3D **9**
Folly Gate *Devn*............................1D **17**
Ford *Devn*.......................................1D **9**
.........................................(nr Bideford)
Ford *Devn*.....................................2C **27**
.......................................(nr Holbeton)
Ford *Devn*....................................2D **29**
.......................................(nr Salcombe)
Ford *Plym*.....................................2A **26**
Ford *Som*......................................1A **12**
Forda *Devn*.....................................3A **4**
Ford Barton *Devn*.........................2D **11**
Forder Green *Devn*.......................1D **27**
Ford Street *Som*...........................2B **12**
Fordton *Devn*................................1C **19**
Forton *Som*...................................3D **13**
Four Lanes *Corn*...........................2D **31**
Fowey *Corn*..................................2B **24**
Foxhole *Corn*................................2D **23**
Fraddam *Corn*...............................2C **31**
Fraddon *Corn*...............................2D **23**
Freathy *Corn*.................................2A **26**
Fremington *Devn*............................3B **4**
Frenchbeer *Devn*..........................2A **18**
Frithelstock *Devn*...........................2D **9**
Frithelstock Stone *Devn*.................2D **9**
Frittiscombe *Devn*.........................3A **28**
Frogmore *Devn*.............................2D **29**
Frogwell *Corn*...............................1D **25**
Fulford *Devn*.................................1C **13**
Fulwood *Som*................................2C **13**
Furley *Devn*..................................3C **13**
Furzehill *Devn*................................2D **5**

Galmington *Som*...........................1C **13**
Galmpton *Devn*.............................2C **29**
Galmpton *Torb*.............................2A **28**
Galmpton Warborough *Torb*.............2A **28**
Gammaton *Devn*............................1D **9**

Gang *Corn*.................................... 1D **25**
Gappah *Devn*............................... 3C **19**
Garras *Corn* ................................ 2B **32**
Georgeham *Devn*........................... 3A **4**
George Nympton *Devn*.................... 1B **10**
Germansweek *Devn*........................ 1C **17**
Germoe *Corn*................................ 3C **31**
Gerrans *Corn*................................ 1C **32**
Gidleigh *Devn*................................ 2A **18**
Gillan *Corn* .................................. 2B **32**
Gittisham *Devn* .............................. 1B **20**
Gluvian *Corn*................................ 1D **23**
Godford Cross *Devn*........................ 3B **12**
Godolphin Cross *Corn* ................... 2D **31**
Golant *Corn*.................................. 2B **24**
Golberdon *Corn*............................ 3B **16**
Goldsithney *Corn*.......................... 2C **31**
Goldworthy *Devn*............................ 1C **8**
Golsoncott *Som*............................. 3C **7**
Goodleigh *Devn*............................. 3C **5**
Goodrington *Torb*.......................... 2A **28**
Goodstone *Devn*............................ 3B **18**
Goonabarn *Corn*........................... 2D **23**
Goonbell *Corn* .............................. 3B **22**
Goonhavern *Corn*.......................... 2B **22**
Goonlaze *Corn*.............................. 1B **32**
Goonvrea *Corn*.............................. 3B **22**
Gooseham *Corn* .............................. 2B **8**
Goosewell *Plym* ............................ 2B **26**
Gorran Churchtown *Corn*................. 3D **23**
Gorran Haven *Corn*........................ 3A **24**
Gorran High Lanes *Corn*................. 3D **23**
Goveton *Devn* .............................. 2D **29**
Grampound *Corn*........................... 3D **23**
Grampound Road *Corn*................... 2D **23**
Gratton *Devn*................................ 2C **8**
Great Bosullow *Corn* ..................... 2B **30**
Great Potheridge *Devn*.................... 2E **9**
Great Torr *Devn* ............................ 2C **29**
Great Torrington *Devn*.................... 2D **9**
Greenbottom *Corn*......................... 3B **22**
Greenham *Som* ............................. 1A **12**
Grenofen *Devn*.............................. 3C **17**
Grimscott *Corn*............................. 3B **8**
Grinacombe Moor *Devn* ................. 1C **17**
Grindhill *Devn* .............................. 1C **17**
Guineaford *Devn*............................ 3B **4**
Gulval *Corn*.................................. 2B **30**
Gulworthy *Devn* ............................ 3C **17**
Gunn *Devn*................................... 3C **5**
Gunnislake *Corn*............................ 3C **17**
Gupworthy *Som*.............................. 3B **6**
Gweek *Corn*................................. 2B **32**
Gwennap *Corn*.............................. 3B **22**
Gwenter *Corn*............................... 3B **32**
Gwinear *Corn*............................... 2C **31**
Gwithian *Corn*............................... 1C **31**

### H

Halberton *Devn*............................. 2A **12**
Halgabron *Corn*............................ 2C **15**
Hallsands *Devn*............................. 3E **29**
Hallspill *Devn*................................ 1D **9**
Hallworthy *Corn* ............................ 2D **15**
Halse *Som*................................... 1B **12**
Halsetown *Corn*............................ 2C **31**

Halsinger *Devn*.............................. 3B **4**
Halsway *Som*................................ 3D **7**
Halwell *Devn*................................. 2D **27**
Halwill *Devn*.................................. 1C **17**
Halwill Junction *Devn*...................... 1C **17**
Ham *Devn*.................................... 3C **13**
Ham *Plym*.................................... 2A **26**
Ham *Som*..................................... 2C **13**
.........................................(nr Ilminster)
Ham *Som*..................................... 1C **13**
..........................................(nr Taunton)
Ham *Som*..................................... 1B **12**
....................................... (nr Wellington)
Hambridge *Som*............................. 1D **13**
Hampton *Devn*.............................. 1C **21**
Hand and Pen *Devn* ...................... 1A **20**
Hannaborough *Devn* ...................... 3E **9**
Hannaford *Devn* ............................ 1A **10**
Harberton *Devn*............................. 2D **27**
Harbertonford *Devn*........................ 2D **27**
Harbourneford *Devn*....................... 1D **27**
Harcombe *Devn* ............................ 1B **20**
Harcombe Bottom *Devn*.................. 1D **21**
Harcourt *Corn* .............................. 1C **32**
Hare *Som*..................................... 2C **13**
Harford *Devn*................................ 2C **27**
Harleston *Devn*.............................. 2D **29**
Harlyn Bay *Corn*............................ 3A **14**
Harpford *Devn*.............................. 1A **20**
Harracott *Devn*.............................. 1E **9**
Harrowbarrow *Corn*........................ 1D **25**
Hartford *Som*................................ 1D **11**
Hartland *Devn*............................... 1B **8**
Hartland Quay *Devn* ...................... 1B **8**
Hartswell *Som*............................... 1A **12**
Hatch Beauchamp *Som*................... 1D **13**
Hatch Green *Som*.......................... 2D **13**
Hatherleigh *Devn*........................... 3E **9**
Hatt *Corn* .................................... 1D **25**
Hawkchurch *Devn*.......................... 3D **13**
Hawkerland *Devn*........................... 2A **20**
Hawkridge *Som* ............................ 3A **6**
Haydon *Som* ................................ 1C **13**
Haye *Corn*.................................... 1D **25**
Hayle *Corn*................................... 2C **31**
Hayne *Devn*.................................. 3C **11**
Haytor Vale *Devn*........................... 3B **18**
Haytown *Devn*............................... 2C **8**
Heale *Devn* .................................. 2C **5**
Heamoor *Corn*.............................. 2B **30**
Heanton Punchardon *Devn*
.................................................. 3B **4**
Heasley Mill *Devn* ......................... 3D **5**
Heath Cross *Devn* ......................... 1B **18**
Heathfield *Devn* ............................ 3C **19**
Heathfield *Som*............................. 3D **7**
................... (nr Lydeard St Lawrence)
Heathfield *Som* ............................ 1B **12**
.............................(nr Norton Fitzwarren)
Heathstock *Devn*........................... 3C **13**
Heavitree *Devn* ............................. 1D **19**
Heddon *Devn*................................ 1A **10**
Hedging *Som*................................ 1D **13**
Hele *Devn*.................................... 3D **11**
..............................................(nr Exeter)
Hele *Devn*.................................... 1B **16**
........................................ (nr Holsworthy)

Hele *Devn*.................................... 2B **4**
...........................................(nr Ilfracombe)
Hele *Torb*.................................... 1B **28**
Helford *Corn*................................ 2B **32**
Helland *Corn*................................ 3C **15**
Helland *Som* ................................ 1D **13**
Hellandbridge *Corn* ....................... 3C **15**
Hellesveor *Corn*............................ 1C **31**
Helston *Corn*................................ 3D **31**
Helstone *Corn*............................... 2C **15**
Hemerdon *Devn*............................ 2B **26**
Hemyock *Devn*.............................. 2B **12**
Hendra *Corn*................................ 2D **23**
Henford *Devn*................................ 1B **16**
Henlade *Som* ................................ 1C **13**
Hennock *Devn*............................... 2C **19**
Henwood *Corn* ............................. 3A **16**
Herner *Devn* ................................. 1E **9**
Herodsfoot *Corn*............................ 1C **25**
Hersham *Corn*............................... 3B **8**
Hessenford *Corn*........................... 2D **25**
Hewas Water *Corn*......................... 3D **23**
Hewood *Dors* ............................... 3D **13**
Hexworthy *Devn*............................ 3A **18**
Heybrook Bay *Devn*........................ 3A **26**
Highampton *Devn* .......................... 3D **9**
High Bickington *Devn*...................... 1A **10**
High Bray *Devn*............................. 3C **5**
High Bullen *Devn* .......................... 1E **9**
Higher Ashton *Devn* ...................... 2C **19**
Higher Bojewyan *Corn*.................... 2A **30**
Higher Cheriton *Devn*..................... 3B **12**
Higher Clovelly *Devn*...................... 1C **8**
Higher Compton *Plym* .................... 2A **26**
Higher Dean *Devn*.......................... 1D **27**
Higher Dunstone *Devn* ................... 3B **18**
Higher Gabwell *Devn*...................... 1B **28**
Higher Porthpean *Corn*................... 2A **24**
Higher Slade *Devn* ........................ 2B **4**
Higher Tale *Devn* .......................... 3A **12**
Higher Town *Som* .......................... 2B **6**
Highertown *Corn*............................ 3C **23**
Higher Vexford *Som* ...................... 3D **7**
Higher Whiteleigh *Corn* .................. 1A **16**
Higher Yalberton *Torb*.................... 2A **28**
High Street *Corn* ........................... 2D **23**
Highweek *Devn*.............................. 3C **19**
Hillcommon *Som*............................ 1B **12**
Hillerton *Devn*............................... 1B **18**
Hillfarrance *Som*............................ 1B **12**
Hillhead *Devn*................................ 2B **28**
Hillside *Devn*................................. 1D **27**
Hiscott *Devn* ................................ 1E **9**
Hittisleigh *Devn*............................. 1B **18**
Hittisleigh Barton *Devn*................... 1B **18**
Hockworthy *Devn*........................... 2A **12**
Hoe, The *Plym* .............................. 2A **26**
Holbeton *Devn*.............................. 2C **27**
Holcombe *Devn*............................. 3D **19**
Holcombe Rogus *Devn*.................... 2A **12**
Holditch *Dors* ............................... 3D **13**
Holemoor *Devn*.............................. 3D **9**
Holford *Som*................................. 2D **7**
Hollacombe *Devn*........................... 3C **8**
Hollocombe *Devn*........................... 2A **10**
Holmacott *Devn* ............................ 1E **9**
Holmbush *Corn*............................. 2A **24**

Holne *Devn* ...................................... 1D **27**
Holsworthy *Devn* .............................. 3C **8**
Holsworthy Beacon *Devn* ................... 3C **8**
Holy City *Devn* ................................. 3D **13**
Holywell *Corn* ................................. 2B **22**
Holywell Lake *Som* ......................... 1B **12**
Honeychurch *Devn* ........................... 3A **10**
Honiton *Devn* ................................. 3B **12**
Hooe *Plym* ..................................... 2B **26**
Hookway *Devn* ................................. 1C **19**
Horn Ash *Dors* ............................... 3D **13**
Horndon *Devn* ................................. 2D **17**
Horner *Som* .................................... 2B **6**
Hornsbury *Som* ............................... 2D **13**
Horns Cross *Devn* ............................ 1C **8**
Horrabridge *Devn* ........................... 1B **26**
Horsebridge *Devn* ........................... 3C **17**
Horton *Som* .................................... 2D **13**
Horton Cross *Som* ........................... 2D **13**
Horwood *Devn* ................................. 1E **9**
Houndsmoor *Som* ........................... 1B **12**
Howleigh *Som* ................................. 2C **13**
Howley *Som* .................................... 3C **13**
Hugus *Corn* .................................... 3B **22**
Huish *Devn* ..................................... 2E **9**
Huish Champflower *Som*
.......................................... 1A **12**
Hulham *Devn* ................................. 2A **20**
Humber *Devn* ................................. 3D **19**
Hungerford *Som* ............................. 2C **7**
Huntham *Som* ................................. 1D **13**
Huntscott *Som* ............................... 2B **6**
Huntsham *Devn* ............................... 1A **12**
Huntshaw *Devn* ............................... 1E **9**
Hurcott *Som* .................................... 2D **13**
Hutcherleigh *Devn* ........................... 2D **27**
Huxham *Devn* ................................. 1D **19**

## I

Iddesleigh *Devn* ............................... 3E **9**
Ide *Devn* ........................................ 1C **19**
Ideford *Devn* ................................. 3C **19**
Idless *Corn* .................................... 3C **23**
Ilford *Som* ...................................... 2D **13**
**Ilfracombe** *Devn* ............................ 2B **4**
Illand *Corn* .................................... 3A **16**
Illogan *Corn* ................................... 3A **22**
Illogan Highway *Corn* ....................... 3A **22**
Ilminster *Som* ................................. 2D **13**
Ilsington *Devn* ................................. 3B **18**
Ilton *Som* ...................................... 2D **13**
Indian Queens *Corn* ......................... 2D **23**
Ingleigh Green *Devn* ......................... 3A **10**
Inner Hope *Devn* ............................. 3C **29**
Instow *Devn* ................................... 3A **4**
Inwardleigh *Devn* ............................ 1D **17**
Ipplepen *Devn* ................................. 1A **28**
Isle Abbotts *Som* ............................. 1D **13**
Isle Brewers *Som* ............................ 1D **13**
Itton *Devn* ...................................... 1A **18**
Ivybridge *Devn* ............................... 2C **27**

## J

Jacobstow *Corn* ............................... 1D **15**
Jacobstowe *Devn* ............................. 3E **9**

## K

Kea *Corn* ........................................ 3C **23**
Keason *Corn* ................................... 1D **25**
Kehelland *Corn* ............................... 3A **22**
Kellacott *Devn* ................................. 2C **17**
Kellaton *Devn* ................................. 3E **29**
Kelly *Devn* ...................................... 2B **16**
Kelly Bray *Corn* ............................... 3B **16**
Kelynack *Corn* ................................. 2A **30**
Kenn *Devn* ...................................... 2D **19**
Kenneggy Downs *Corn* ....................... 3C **31**
Kennerleigh *Devn* ............................ 3C **11**
Kennford *Devn* ................................. 2D **19**
Kentisbeare *Devn* ............................. 3A **12**
Kentisbury *Devn* ............................... 2C **5**
Kentisbury Ford *Devn* ........................ 2C **5**
Kenton *Devn* ................................... 2D **19**
Kenwyn *Corn* ................................... 3C **23**
Kerris *Corn* ..................................... 3B **30**
Kersbrook *Devn* ............................... 2A **20**
Kerswell *Devn* ................................. 3A **12**
Kestle *Corn* .................................... 3D **23**
Kestle Mill *Corn* ............................... 2C **23**
Kilkhampton *Corn* ............................ 2B **8**
Kilmington *Devn* ............................. 1C **21**
Kilton *Som* ...................................... 2D **7**
Kilve *Som* ...................................... 2D **7**
Kingsand *Corn* ................................. 2A **26**
Kingsbridge *Som* ............................. 3B **6**
Kingsbridge *Devn* ............................ 2D **29**
Kingscott *Devn* ............................... 2E **9**
Kingsheanton *Devn* .......................... 3B **4**
Kingskerswell *Devn* .......................... 1A **28**
King's Nympton *Devn* ........................ 2A **10**
Kingsteignton *Devn* .......................... 3C **19**
Kingston *Devn* ................................. 2C **29**
Kingstone *Som* ............................... 2D **13**
Kingston St Mary *Som*
.......................................... 1C **13**
Kingswear *Devn* ............................... 2A **28**
Kingswood *Som* ............................... 3D **7**
Kittisford *Som* ................................. 1A **12**
Knapp *Som* .................................... 1D **13**
Knightacott *Devn* ............................ 3C **5**
Knighton *Devn* ................................. 3B **26**
Knighton *Som* ................................. 2D **7**
Knowle *Devn* ................................... 3A **4**
.............................. (nr Braunton)
Knowle *Devn* ................................... 2A **20**
...................... (nr Budleigh Salterton)
Knowle *Devn* ................................... 3B **10**
.............................. (nr Crediton)
Knowle St Giles *Som* ......................... 2D **13**
Knowstone *Devn* ............................. 1C **11**
Kuggar *Corn* ................................... 3B **32**

## L

Ladock *Corn* ................................... 2C **23**
Ladycross *Corn* ............................... 2B **16**
Lake *Devn* ...................................... 3B **4**
Lamellion *Corn* ............................... 1C **25**
Lamerton *Devn* ............................... 3C **17**
Lamorick *Corn* ............................... 1A **24**
Lamorna *Corn* ................................. 3B **30**
Lamorran *Corn* ............................... 3C **23**

Lana *Devn* ...................................... 1B **16**
.............................. (nr Ashwater)
Lana *Devn* ...................................... 3C **8**
.............................. (nr Holsworthy)
Lanarth *Corn* ................................. 2B **32**
Landcross *Devn* ............................... 1D **9**
Landkey *Devn* ................................. 3B **4**
Landkey Newland *Devn* ..................... 3B **4**
Landrake *Corn* ............................... 1D **25**
Landscove *Devn* ............................. 1D **27**
Land's End Airport *Corn* ..................... 3A **30**
Landulph *Corn* ............................... 1A **26**
Lane *Corn* ...................................... 1C **23**
Laneast *Corn* ................................. 2A **16**
Langdon *Corn* ................................. 1A **16**
Langdon Cross *Corn* ......................... 2B **16**
Langford *Devn* ............................... 3A **12**
Langford *Som* ................................. 1C **13**
Langford Budville *Som* ....................... 1B **12**
Langley *Som* ................................... 1A **12**
Langley Marsh *Som* .......................... 1A **12**
Langore *Corn* ................................. 2A **16**
Langridgeford *Devn* .......................... 1E **9**
Langtree *Devn* ............................... 2D **9**
Lanivet *Corn* ................................... 1A **24**
Lanjeth *Corn* ................................. 2D **23**
Lank *Corn* ...................................... 3C **15**
Lanlivery *Corn* ............................... 2A **24**
Lanner *Corn* ................................... 1B **32**
Lanreath *Corn* ............................... 2B **24**
Lansallos *Corn* ............................... 2B **24**
Lanteglos Highway *Corn* ................... 2B **24**
Lapford *Devn* ................................. 3B **10**
Lapford Cross *Devn* .......................... 3B **10**
Latchley *Corn* ................................. 3C **17**
Launcells *Corn* ............................... 3B **8**
Launceston *Corn* ............................. 2B **16**
Lawhitton *Corn* ............................... 2B **16**
Laymore *Dors* ................................. 3D **13**
Ledstone *Devn* ............................... 2D **29**
Lee *Devn* ...................................... 2A **4**
.............................. (nr Ilfracombe)
Lee *Devn* ...................................... 1C **11**
.............................. (nr South Molton)
Leedstown *Corn* ............................. 2D **31**
Lee Mill *Devn* ................................. 2B **26**
Lee Moor *Devn* ............................... 1B **26**
Leigham *Plym* ............................... 2B **26**
Leighland Chapel *Som* ....................... 3C **7**
Lelant *Corn* .................................... 2C **31**
Lelant Downs *Corn* .......................... 2C **31**
Lerryn *Corn* .................................... 2B **24**
Lesnewth *Corn* ............................... 1D **15**
Lettaford *Devn* ............................... 2B **18**
Leusdon *Devn* ................................. 3B **18**
Lewannick *Corn* ............................. 2A **16**
Lewdown *Devn* ............................... 2C **17**
Leworthy *Devn* ............................... 3C **5**
.............................. (nr Barnstaple)
Leworthy *Devn* ............................... 3C **8**
.............................. (nr Holsworthy)
Lewthorn Cross *Devn* ....................... 3B **18**
Lewtrenchard *Devn* .......................... 2C **17**
Ley *Corn* ........................................ 1B **24**
Lezant *Corn* ................................... 3B **16**
Liddaton *Devn* ............................... 2C **17**
Lifton *Devn* .................................... 2B **16**

| | | |
|---|---|---|
| Liftondown *Devn* | 2B **16** | |
| Lillesdon *Som* | 1D **13** | |
| Lilstock *Som* | 2D **7** | |
| Linkinhorne *Corn* | 3B **16** | |
| Liscombe *Som* | 3A **6** | |
| Liskeard *Corn* | 1C **25** | |
| Littleborough *Devn* | 2C **11** | |
| Littleham *Devn* | 1D **9** | |
| (nr Bideford) | | |
| Littleham *Devn* | 2A **20** | |
| (nr Exmouth) | | |
| Littlehempston *Devn* | 1A **28** | |
| Little Petherick *Corn* | 3B **14** | |
| Little Potheridge *Devn* | 2E **9** | |
| Little Torrington *Devn* | 2D **9** | |
| Liverton *Devn* | 3C **19** | |
| Lizard *Corn* | 3B **32** | |
| Lobb *Devn* | 3A **4** | |
| Lobhillcross *Devn* | 2C **17** | |
| Lockengate *Corn* | 1A **24** | |
| Loddiswell *Devn* | 2D **29** | |
| London Apprentice *Corn* | 2A **24** | |
| Longdown *Devn* | 1C **19** | |
| Longdowns *Corn* | 1B **32** | |
| Longrock *Corn* | 2C **31** | |
| Looe *Corn* | 2C **25** | |
| Lostwithiel *Corn* | 2B **24** | |
| Lower Amble *Corn* | 3B **14** | |
| Lower Ashton *Devn* | 2C **19** | |
| Lower Cheriton *Devn* | 3B **12** | |
| Lower Dean *Devn* | 1D **27** | |
| Lower Gabwell *Devn* | 1B **28** | |
| Lower Holditch *Dors* | 3D **13** | |
| Lower Lovacott *Devn* | 1E **9** | |
| Lower Loxhore *Devn* | 3C **5** | |
| Lower Slade *Devn* | 2B **4** | |
| Lower Tale *Devn* | 3A **12** | |
| Lowertown *Corn* | 3D **31** | |
| Lower Vexford *Som* | 3D **7** | |
| Lower Wear *Devn* | 2D **19** | |
| Lowton *Devn* | 3A **10** | |
| Lowton *Som* | 2B **12** | |
| Loxbeare *Devn* | 2D **11** | |
| Loxhore *Devn* | 3C **5** | |
| Luccombe *Som* | 2B **6** | |
| Luckett *Corn* | 3B **16** | |
| Luckwell Bridge *Som* | 3B **6** | |
| Ludgvan *Corn* | 2C **31** | |
| Luffincott *Devn* | 1B **16** | |
| Luppitt *Devn* | 3B **12** | |
| Lupridge *Devn* | 2D **27** | |
| Lurley *Devn* | 2D **11** | |
| Luscombe *Devn* | 2D **27** | |
| Luson *Devn* | 2C **29** | |
| Lustleigh *Devn* | 2B **18** | |
| Luton *Devn* | 3A **12** | |
| (nr Honiton) | | |
| Luton *Devn* | 3D **19** | |
| (nr Teignmouth) | | |
| Lutton *Devn* | 2B **26** | |
| (nr Ivybridge) | | |
| Lutton *Devn* | 1C **27** | |
| (nr South Brent) | | |
| Lutworthy *Devn* | 2B **10** | |
| Luxborough *Som* | 3B **6** | |
| Luxulyan *Corn* | 2A **24** | |
| Lydcott *Devn* | 3C **5** | |

| | | |
|---|---|---|
| Lydeard St Lawrence *Som* | 3D **7** | |
| Lydford *Devn* | 2D **17** | |
| Lydmarsh *Som* | 3D **13** | |
| Lyme Regis *Dors* | 1D **21** | |
| Lympstone *Devn* | 2D **19** | |
| Lynbridge *Devn* | 2D **5** | |
| Lynch *Som* | 2B **6** | |
| Lynmouth *Devn* | 2D **5** | |
| Lynstone *Corn* | 3B **8** | |
| Lynton *Devn* | 2D **5** | |

## M

| | | |
|---|---|---|
| Mabe Burnthouse *Corn* | 1B **32** | |
| Madford *Devn* | 2B **12** | |
| Madron *Corn* | 2B **30** | |
| Maenporth *Corn* | 2B **32** | |
| Maidencombe *Torb* | 1B **28** | |
| Maidenhayne *Devn* | 1C **21** | |
| Maidenwell *Corn* | 3D **15** | |
| Malborough *Devn* | 3D **29** | |
| Malmsmead *Devn* | 2D **5** | |
| Malpas *Corn* | 3C **23** | |
| Manaccan *Corn* | 2B **32** | |
| Manaton *Devn* | 2B **18** | |
| Marazion *Corn* | 2C **31** | |
| Marhamchurch *Corn* | 3B **8** | |
| Mariansleigh *Devn* | 1B **10** | |
| Markwell *Corn* | 2D **25** | |
| Marldon *Devn* | 1A **28** | |
| Marsh *Devn* | 2C **13** | |
| Marshalsea *Dors* | 3D **13** | |
| Marshgate *Corn* | 1D **15** | |
| Marsh Green *Devn* | 1A **20** | |
| Marsh Street *Som* | 2B **6** | |
| Marshwood *Dors* | 1D **21** | |
| Martinhoe *Devn* | 2C **5** | |
| Martinhoe Cross *Devn* | 2C **5** | |
| Marwood *Devn* | 3B **4** | |
| Maryfield *Corn* | 2A **26** | |
| Marystow *Devn* | 2C **17** | |
| Mary Tavy *Devn* | 3D **17** | |
| Maudlin *Corn* | 1A **24** | |
| Mawgan *Corn* | 2B **32** | |
| Mawgan Porth *Corn* | 1C **23** | |
| Mawla *Corn* | 3B **22** | |
| Mawnan *Corn* | 2B **32** | |
| Mawnan Smith *Corn* | 2B **32** | |
| Maxworthy *Corn* | 1A **16** | |
| Mead *Devn* | 2B **8** | |
| Meadwell *Devn* | 2C **17** | |
| Meare Green *Som* | 1C **13** | |
| (nr Curry Mallet) | | |
| Meare Green *Som* | 1D **13** | |
| (nr Stoke St Gregory) | | |
| Meavy *Devn* | 1B **26** | |
| Meddon *Devn* | 2B **8** | |
| Meeth *Devn* | 3E **9** | |
| Meldon *Devn* | 1D **17** | |
| Membury *Devn* | 3C **13** | |
| Menabilly *Corn* | 2A **24** | |
| Menheniot *Corn* | 1C **25** | |
| Menna *Corn* | 2D **23** | |
| Merrivale *Devn* | 3D **17** | |
| Merryfield Airfield *Som* | 2D **13** | |
| Merrymeet *Corn* | 1C **25** | |
| Merther *Corn* | 3C **23** | |

| | | |
|---|---|---|
| Merton *Devn* | 2E **9** | |
| Meshaw *Devn* | 2B **10** | |
| Metcombe *Devn* | 1A **20** | |
| Metherell *Corn* | 1A **26** | |
| Mevagissey *Corn* | 3A **24** | |
| Michaelstow *Corn* | 3C **15** | |
| Michelcombe *Devn* | 1C **27** | |
| Middlecott *Devn* | 2B **18** | |
| Middle Marwood *Devn* | 3B **4** | |
| Middlemoor *Devn* | 3C **17** | |
| Middle Taphouse *Corn* | 1B **24** | |
| Middlewood *Corn* | 3A **16** | |
| Milford *Devn* | 1B **8** | |
| Millbrook *Corn* | 2A **26** | |
| Millhayes *Devn* | 3C **13** | |
| (nr Honiton) | | |
| Millhayes *Devn* | 2B **12** | |
| (nr Wellington) | | |
| Millpool *Corn* | 3D **15** | |
| Milltown *Corn* | 2B **24** | |
| Milltown *Devn* | 3B **4** | |
| Milton Abbot *Devn* | 3C **17** | |
| Milton Combe *Devn* | 1A **26** | |
| Milton Damerel *Devn* | 2C **8** | |
| Milton Hill *Devn* | 3D **19** | |
| Milverton *Som* | 1B **12** | |
| Minehead *Som* | 2B **6** | |
| Minions *Corn* | 3A **16** | |
| Mitchell *Corn* | 2C **23** | |
| Mithian *Corn* | 2B **22** | |
| Modbury *Devn* | 2C **27** | |
| Mogworthy *Devn* | 2C **11** | |
| Molland *Devn* | 1C **11** | |
| Monkleigh *Devn* | 1D **9** | |
| Monkokehampton *Devn* | 3E **9** | |
| Monksilver *Som* | 3C **7** | |
| Monkton *Devn* | 3B **12** | |
| Monkton Heathfield *Som* | 1C **13** | |
| Monkton Wyld *Dors* | 1D **21** | |
| Moor Cross *Devn* | 2C **27** | |
| Moortown *Devn* | 1B **16** | |
| Morchard Bishop *Devn* | 3B **10** | |
| Morebath *Devn* | 1D **11** | |
| Moreleigh *Devn* | 2D **27** | |
| Moretonhampstead *Devn* | 2B **18** | |
| Mortehoe *Devn* | 2A **4** | |
| Morval *Corn* | 2B **30** | |
| Morval *Corn* | 2C **25** | |
| Morwenstow *Corn* | 2B **8** | |
| Mothecombe *Devn* | 2C **29** | |
| Mount *Corn* | 1B **24** | |
| (nr Bodmin) | | |
| Mount *Corn* | 2B **22** | |
| (nr Newquay) | | |
| Mount Ambrose *Corn* | 3B **22** | |
| Mount Hawke *Corn* | 3B **22** | |
| Mountjoy *Corn* | 1C **23** | |
| Mousehole *Corn* | 3B **30** | |
| Muchlarnick *Corn* | 2C **25** | |
| Muddiford *Devn* | 3B **4** | |
| Mullacott *Devn* | 2B **4** | |
| Mullion *Corn* | 3A **32** | |
| Mullion Cove *Corn* | 3A **32** | |
| Murchington *Devn* | 2A **18** | |
| Musbury *Devn* | 1C **21** | |
| Mutterton *Devn* | 3A **12** | |
| Mylor Bridge *Corn* | 1C **32** | |

Mylor Churchtown *Corn* .................. 1C **32**

### N

Nailsbourne *Som* ............................ 1C **13**
Nancegollan *Corn*........................... 2D **31**
Nancledra *Corn*.............................. 2B **30**
Nanpean *Corn*................................ 2D **23**
Nanstallon *Corn* ............................ 1A **24**
Narkurs *Corn* ................................ 2D **25**
Natcott *Devn*.................................... 1B **8**
Nethercott *Devn*.............................. 3A **4**
Nether Exe *Devn*............................. 3D **11**
Nether Stowey *Som* ........................ 3D **7**
Netherton *Devn*.............................. 3C **19**
Netton *Devn*................................... 3B **26**
Newbridge *Corn*............................. 2B **30**
Newbuildings *Devn*......................... 3B **10**
Newcott *Devn*................................ 3C **13**
Newland *Som* ................................ 3A **6**
Newlyn *Corn*.................................. 3B **30**
New Mill *Corn*............................... 2B **30**
New Mills *Corn* ............................. 2C **23**
New Polzeath *Corn*......................... 3B **14**
Newport *Corn*................................ 2B **16**
Newport *Devn*................................. 3B **4**
Newport *Som*................................. 1D **13**
**Newquay** *Corn* ........................... 1C **23**
Newquay Cornwall Airport *Corn* ........ 1C **23**
Newton *Som*.................................... 3D **7**
**Newton Abbot** *Devn*...................... 3C **19**
Newton Ferrers *Devn* ...................... 3B **26**
Newton Poppleford *Devn*................ 2A **20**
Newton St Cyres *Devn* .................... 1C **19**
Newton St Petrock *Devn* .................. 2D **9**
Newton Tracey *Devn*........................ 1E **9**
Newtown *Corn*............................... 3A **16**
Newtown *Devn*............................... 1B **10**
Newtown *Som* ............................... 2C **13**
Newtown-in-St Martin *Corn* .............. 2B **32**
Nicholashayne *Devn*........................ 2B **12**
Nightcott *Som*................................ 1C **11**
Nimmer *Som*.................................. 2D **13**
Nomansland *Devn*........................... 2C **11**
Norman's Green *Devn*...................... 3A **12**
Northam *Devn*................................. 1D **9**
Northay *Som*.................................. 2C **13**
North Bovey *Devn* .......................... 2B **18**
North Brentor *Devn*......................... 2C **17**
North Buckland *Devn* ........................ 2A **4**
North Coombe *Devn*........................ 2C **11**
Northcott *Devn*............................... 1B **16**
.................................(nr Boyton)
Northcott *Devn*............................... 2A **12**
.................................(nr Culmstock)
North Curry *Som*............................ 1D **13**
North Heasley *Devn* ........................ 3D **5**
North Hill *Corn* .............................. 3A **16**
North Huish *Devn*........................... 2D **27**
Northleigh *Devn*.............................. 3C **5**
.................................(nr Barnstaple)
Northleigh *Devn*.............................. 1B **20**
................................. (nr Honiton)
Northlew *Devn*................................ 1D **17**
North Molton *Devn*.......................... 1B **10**
North Petherwin *Corn*...................... 2A **16**
North Radworthy *Devn*...................... 3D **5**

North Tamerton *Corn* ...................... 1B **16**
North Tawton *Devn*.......................... 3A **10**
North Town *Devn*.............................. 3E **9**
North Whilborough *Devn*................. 1A **28**
Norton *Devn*................................... 2A **28**
Norton Fitzwarren *Som* .................... 1C **13**
Noss Mayo *Devn*............................ 3B **26**
Nymet Rowland *Devn*....................... 3B **10**
Nymet Tracey *Devn*......................... 3B **10**
Nynehead *Som* .............................. 1B **12**

### O

Oake *Som*...................................... 1B **12**
Oakford *Devn*................................. 1D **11**
Oakfordbridge *Devn*........................ 1D **11**
Oare *Som*........................................ 2A **6**
Oareford *Som* .................................. 2A **6**
Oath *Som*...................................... 1D **13**
Offwell *Devn*.................................. 1B **20**
Okehampton *Devn*.......................... 1D **17**
Okehampton Camp *Devn* ................ 1D **17**
Oldborough *Devn*........................... 3B **10**
Old Cleeve *Som* ............................. 2C **7**
Old Kea *Corn*................................. 3C **23**
Old Mill *Corn*................................ 3B **16**
Oldridge *Devn*................................ 1C **19**
Oldways End *Som*........................... 1C **11**
Orchard Hill *Devn*............................. 1D **9**
Orchard Portman *Som* ..................... 1C **13**
Otterford *Som*................................ 2C **13**
Otterham *Corn*............................... 1D **15**
Otterton *Devn*................................ 2A **20**
Ottery St Mary *Devn*....................... 1A **20**
Outer Hope *Devn*............................ 2C **29**
Over Stowey *Som* ........................... 3D **7**

### P

Padson *Devn*.................................. 1D **17**
Padstow *Corn*................................. 3B **14**
**Paignton** *Torb*............................ 1A **28**
Pancrasweek *Devn*............................ 3B **8**
Par *Corn* ....................................... 2A **24**
Park Bottom *Corn*........................... 3A **22**
Parkfield *Corn*................................ 1D **25**
Parkham *Devn*................................. 1C **8**
Parkham Ash *Devn* ........................... 1C **8**
Parracombe *Devn*............................ 2C **5**
Patchacott *Devn*............................. 1C **17**
Patchole *Devn*................................ 2C **5**
Pathfinder Village *Devn*.................... 1C **19**
Paul *Corn*...................................... 3B **30**
Payhembury *Devn*........................... 3A **12**
Payton *Som*................................... 1B **12**
Peasmarsh *Som*............................. 2D **13**
Pelynt *Corn*................................... 2C **25**
Penare *Corn*................................... 3D **23**
Penbeagle *Corn* ............................. 2C **31**
Penberth *Corn*................................ 3B **30**
Pencarrow *Corn*............................. 2D **15**
Pendeen *Corn*................................ 2A **30**
Pendoggett *Corn*............................ 3C **15**
Penelewey *Corn*............................. 3C **23**
Pengelly *Corn*................................ 2C **15**
Pengersick *Corn*............................ 3C **31**
Pengover Green *Corn*....................... 1C **25**

Penhale *Corn* ................................. 3A **32**
................................(nr Mullion)
Penhale *Corn* ................................. 2D **23**
................................(nr St Austell)
Penhale Camp *Corn*........................ 2B **22**
Penhallow *Corn*.............................. 2B **22**
Penhalvean *Corn*............................ 1B **32**
Penmarth *Corn*............................... 1B **32**
Penn *Dors*..................................... 1D **21**
Pennsylvania *Devn*.......................... 1D **19**
Pennycross *Plym*............................ 2A **26**
Pennymoor *Devn*............................ 2C **11**
Penpillick *Corn*............................... 2A **24**
Penpol *Corn*.................................. 1C **32**
Penpoll *Corn*................................. 2B **24**
Penponds *Corn*.............................. 2D **31**
Penpont *Corn*................................ 3C **15**
Penquit *Devn* ................................ 2C **27**
Penrose *Corn*................................. 3A **14**
Penryn *Corn*.................................. 1B **32**
Pensilva *Corn*................................. 1C **25**
Penstone *Devn*............................... 3B **10**
Pentewan *Corn*............................... 3A **24**
Pentire *Corn*.................................. 1B **22**
Penwithick *Corn*............................. 2A **24**
**Penzance** *Corn*........................... 2B **30**
Periton *Som*.................................... 2B **6**
Perranarworthal *Corn*...................... 1B **32**
Perranporth *Corn* ........................... 2B **22**
Perranporth Airfield *Corn*................. 2B **22**
Perranuthnoe *Corn*......................... 3C **31**
Perranwell *Corn* ............................. 1B **32**
Perranzabuloe *Corn*........................ 2B **22**
Perry Street *Som* ........................... 3D **13**
Peters Marland *Devn*........................ 2D **9**
Peter Tavy *Devn*............................. 3D **17**
Petherwin Gate *Corn*........................ 2A **16**
Petrockstowe *Devn*........................... 3E **9**
Petton *Devn*................................... 1A **12**
Philham *Devn*.................................... 1B **8**
Phillack *Corn*................................. 2C **31**
Philleigh *Corn* ............................... 1C **32**
Pickwell *Devn*.................................. 2A **4**
Pillaton *Corn*.................................. 1D **25**
Pinhoe *Devn*.................................. 1D **19**
Pipers Pool *Corn* ........................... 2A **16**
Pippacott *Devn*................................. 3B **4**
Pitminster *Som*............................... 2C **13**
Pitsford Hill *Som*.............................. 3D **7**
Pityme *Corn*.................................. 3B **14**
Plaidy *Corn* ................................... 2C **25**
Plainsfield *Som*................................ 3D **7**
Playing Place *Corn*.......................... 3C **23**
Plushabridge *Corn*.......................... 3B **16**
**Plymouth** *Plym*.................... 35 (2A **26**)
Plympton *Plym*............................... 2B **26**
Plymstock *Plym* ............................. 2B **26**
Plymtree *Devn* ............................... 3A **12**
Polbathic *Corn* .............................. 2D **25**
Polbrock *Corn*................................ 1A **24**
Polgooth *Corn*................................ 2D **23**
Polkerris *Corn*................................ 2A **24**
Polmassick *Corn*............................ 3D **23**
Polperro *Corn*................................ 2C **25**
Polruan *Corn*................................. 2B **24**
Polscoe *Corn*................................. 1B **24**
Poltesco *Corn*................................ 3B **32**

Poltimore *Devn* .................................. 1D **19**
Polyphant *Corn* ................................ 2A **16**
Polzeath *Corn*.................................... 3B **14**
Ponsanooth *Corn*.............................. 1B **32**
Ponsongath *Corn* ............................. 3B **32**
Ponsworthy *Devn* ............................. 3B **18**
Pool *Corn*........................................... 3A **22**
Poole *Som* ........................................ 1B **12**
Porkellis *Corn*.................................... 2D **31**
Porlock *Som* ....................................... 2A **6**
Porlock Weir *Som* ............................... 2A **6**
Portgate *Devn*................................... 2C **17**
Port Gaverne *Corn*............................ 2C **15**
Porth *Corn* ........................................ 1C **23**
Porthallow *Corn* ................................ 2C **25**
.......................................... (nr Looe)
Porthallow *Corn* ................................ 2B **32**
.................................. (nr St Keverne)
Porthcothan *Corn*.............................. 3A **14**
Porthcurno *Corn*................................ 3A **30**
Porthgwarra *Corn*.............................. 3A **30**
Porthleven *Corn* ................................ 3D **31**
Porthmeor *Corn*................................. 2B **30**
Porth Navas *Corn*.............................. 2B **32**
Portholland *Corn* ............................... 3D **23**
Porthoustock *Corn* ............................ 2C **32**
Porthtowan *Corn*............................... 3A **22**
Port Isaac *Corn*................................. 2B **14**
Portloe *Corn*...................................... 1D **33**
Portmellon *Corn*................................ 3A **24**
Port Quin *Corn* ................................. 2B **14**
Portreath *Corn* .................................. 3A **22**
Portscatho *Corn*................................ 1C **32**
Portwrinkle *Corn*................................ 2D **25**
Postbridge *Devn*................................ 3A **18**
Poughill *Corn* ..................................... 3B **8**
Poughill *Devn*.................................... 3C **11**
Poundsgate *Devn*.............................. 3B **18**
Poundstock *Corn*............................... 1A **16**
Powderham *Devn*.............................. 2D **19**
Praa Sands *Corn*............................... 3C **31**
Praze-an-Beeble *Corn*....................... 2D **31**
Predannack Airfield *Corn*................... 3A **32**
Prescott *Devn* ................................... 2A **12**
Preston *Devn* .................................... 3C **19**
Preston Bowyer *Som*......................... 1B **12**
Princetown *Devn*................................ 3D **17**
Prixford *Devn*...................................... 3B **4**
Probus *Corn*...................................... 3C **23**
Puckington *Som*................................. 2D **13**
Puddington *Devn*............................... 2C **11**
Purtington *Som*.................................. 3D **13**
Putsborough *Devn*.............................. 2A **4**
Pyworthy *Devn*.................................... 3C **8**

### Q

Queen Dart *Devn* .............................. 2C **11**
Quethiock *Corn*.................................. 1D **25**
Quintrell Downs *Corn*........................ 1C **23**
Quoditch *Devn*................................... 1C **17**

### R

Rackenford *Devn* ............................... 2C **11**
Rame *Corn*......................................... 3A **26**
.......................................... (nr Millbrook)

Rame *Corn*........................................ 1B **32**
.......................................... (nr Penryn)
Ramsley *Devn*.................................... 1A **18**
Rapps *Som* ....................................... 2D **13**
Rattery *Devn*...................................... 1D **27**
Rawridge *Devn* .................................. 3C **13**
Raymond's Hill *Devn*.......................... 1D **21**
Readymoney *Corn*.............................. 2B **24**
Redgate *Corn*.................................... 1C **25**
Red Post *Corn*..................................... 3B **8**
**Redruth** *Corn* ................................ 3B **22**
Rejerrah *Corn*.................................... 2B **22**
Releath *Corn*..................................... 2D **31**
Relubbus *Corn*.................................. 2C **31**
Rescassa *Corn*................................... 3D **23**
Rescorla *Corn* ................................... 2A **24**
.................................. (nr Penwithick)
Rescorla *Corn* ................................... 3D **23**
.......................................... (nr Sticker)
Retire *Corn*........................................ 1A **24**
Rew *Devn*.......................................... 3D **29**
Rewe *Devn*........................................ 1D **19**
Rexon *Devn* ...................................... 2C **17**
Rezare *Corn*...................................... 3B **16**
Rickham *Devn*.................................... 3D **29**
Riddlecombe *Devn*............................. 2A **10**
Rilla Mill *Corn* ................................... 3A **16**
Ringmore *Devn*.................................. 2C **29**
.................................. (nr Kingsbridge)
Ringmore *Devn*.................................. 3D **19**
.................................. (nr Teignmouth)
Rinsey *Corn*....................................... 3C **31**
Roachill *Devn*.................................... 1C **11**
Roadwater *Som* ................................... 3C **7**
Roborough *Devn* .................................. 2E **9**
.............................. (nr Great Torrington)
Roborough *Devn*................................ 1B **26**
.......................................... (nr Plymouth)
Roche *Corn*....................................... 1D **23**
Rock *Corn*......................................... 3B **14**
Rockbeare *Devn*................................ 1A **20**
Rockhead *Corn* ................................. 2C **15**
Rockwell Green *Som*.......................... 2B **12**
Rodhuish *Som* ..................................... 3C **7**
Romansleigh *Devn*............................. 1B **10**
Rook's Nest *Som* ................................. 3C **7**
Rose *Corn*......................................... 2B **22**
Rose Ash *Devn*.................................. 1B **10**
Rosemary Lane *Devn*......................... 2B **12**
Rosenannon *Corn*.............................. 1D **23**
Rosevean *Corn*.................................. 2A **24**
Roseworthy *Corn* .............................. 2D **31**
Roskorwell *Corn*................................ 2B **32**
Rosudgeon *Corn* ............................... 3C **31**
Round Hill *Torb*.................................. 1A **28**
Rousdon *Devn*................................... 1C **21**
Row *Corn*.......................................... 3C **15**
Rowden *Devn*.................................... 1A **18**
Royston Water *Som* ........................... 2C **13**
Ruan High Lanes *Corn* ...................... 1D **33**
Ruan Lanihorne *Corn* ........................ 3C **23**
Ruan Major *Corn*............................... 3B **32**
Ruan Minor *Corn*............................... 3B **32**
Ruishton *Som* .................................... 1C **13**
Rumford *Corn* ................................... 3A **14**
Rumwell *Som* .................................... 1B **12**
Rundlestone *Devn*.............................. 3D **17**

Runnington *Som* ................................ 1B **12**
Rushford *Devn*................................... 3C **17**
Ruthernbridge *Corn*........................... 1A **24**
Ruthvoes *Corn* .................................. 1D **23**

### S

St Agnes *Corn*................................... 2B **22**
St Allen *Corn*..................................... 2C **23**
St Ann's Chapel *Corn*........................ 3C **17**
St Ann's Chapel *Devn* ....................... 2C **29**
St Anthony *Corn*................................ 1C **32**
St Anthony-in-Meneage *Corn*............ 2B **32**
**St Austell** *Corn*.............................. 2A **24**
St Blazey *Corn* .................................. 2A **24**
St Blazey Gate *Corn*.......................... 2A **24**
St Breock *Corn*.................................. 3B **14**
St Breward *Corn* ............................... 3C **15**
St Budeaux *Plym*............................... 2A **26**
St Buryan *Corn* ................................. 3B **30**
St Cleer *Corn* .................................... 1C **25**
St Clement *Corn*................................ 3C **23**
St Clether *Corn* ................................. 2A **16**
St Columb Major *Corn*....................... 1D **23**
St Columb Minor *Corn*....................... 1C **23**
St Columb Road *Corn*........................ 2D **23**
St Day *Corn* ...................................... 3B **22**
St Dennis *Corn*.................................. 2D **23**
St Dominick *Corn*.............................. 1D **25**
St Endellion *Corn* .............................. 3B **14**
St Enoder *Corn*.................................. 2C **23**
St Erme *Corn* .................................... 3C **23**
St Erney *Corn*.................................... 2D **25**
St Erth *Corn* ...................................... 2C **31**
St Erth Praze *Corn* ........................... 2C **31**
St Ervan *Corn*.................................... 3A **14**
St Eval *Corn*...................................... 1C **23**
St Ewe *Corn*...................................... 3D **23**
St Gennys *Corn*................................. 1D **15**
St Germans *Corn* .............................. 2D **25**
St Giles in the Wood *Devn*.................. 2E **9**
St Giles on the Heath *Devn* ............... 1B **16**
St Gluvias *Corn*................................. 1B **32**
St Hilary *Corn*.................................... 2C **31**
Saint Hill *Devn* .................................. 3A **12**
St Issey *Corn* .................................... 3B **14**
St Ive *Corn*........................................ 1D **25**
**St Ives** *Corn* ................................. 1C **31**
St Jidgey *Corn* .................................. 1D **23**
St John *Corn*..................................... 2A **26**
St John's Chapel *Devn*....................... 1E **9**
St Just *Corn*...................................... 2A **30**
St Just in Roseland *Corn*................... 1C **32**
St Keverne *Corn*................................ 2B **32**
St Kew *Corn*...................................... 3C **15**
St Kew Highway *Corn* ........................ 3C **15**
St Keyne *Corn*................................... 1C **25**
St Lawrence *Corn* ............................. 1A **24**
St Levan *Corn*................................... 3A **30**
St Mabyn *Corn*.................................. 3C **15**
St Martin *Corn* .................................. 2B **32**
.......................................... (nr Helston)
St Martin *Corn* .................................. 2C **25**
.......................................... (nr Looe)
St Marychurch *Torb*........................... 1B **28**
St Mawes *Corn*.................................. 1C **32**
St Mawgan *Corn*................................ 1C **23**

| | |
|---|---|
| St Mellion *Corn* | 1D **25** |
| St Merryn *Corn* | 3A **14** |
| St Mewan *Corn* | 2D **23** |
| St Michael Caerhays *Corn* | 3D **23** |
| St Michael Penkevil *Corn* | 3C **23** |
| St Michaels *Torb* | 2A **28** |
| St Minver *Corn* | 3B **14** |
| St Neot *Corn* | 1B **24** |
| St Newlyn East *Corn* | 2C **23** |
| St Pinnock *Corn* | 1C **25** |
| St Ruan *Corn* | 3B **32** |
| St Stephen *Corn* | 2D **23** |
| St Stephens *Corn* | 2B **16** |
| (nr Launceston) | |
| St Stephens *Corn* | 2A **26** |
| (nr Saltash) | |
| St Teath *Corn* | 2C **15** |
| St Thomas *Devn* | 1D **19** |
| St Tudy *Corn* | 3C **15** |
| St Veep *Corn* | 2B **24** |
| St Wenn *Corn* | 1D **23** |
| St Winnolls *Corn* | 2D **25** |
| St Winnow *Corn* | 2B **24** |
| Salcombe *Devn* | 3D **29** |
| Salcombe Regis *Devn* | 2B **20** |
| Saltash *Corn* | 2A **26** |
| Saltrens *Devn* | 1D **9** |
| Sampford Arundel *Som* | 2B **12** |
| Sampford Brett *Som* | 2C **7** |
| Sampford Courtenay *Devn* | 3A **10** |
| Sampford Peverell *Devn* | 2A **12** |
| Sampford Spiney *Devn* | 3D **17** |
| Sancreed *Corn* | 3B **30** |
| Sandford *Devn* | 3C **11** |
| Sandplace *Corn* | 2C **25** |
| Sandygate *Devn* | 3C **19** |
| Satterleigh *Devn* | 1A **10** |
| Saunton *Devn* | 3A **4** |
| Scorrier *Corn* | 3B **22** |
| Scorriton *Devn* | 1D **27** |
| Sea *Som* | 2D **13** |
| Seaton *Corn* | 2D **25** |
| Seaton *Devn* | 1C **21** |
| Seaton Junction *Devn* | 1C **21** |
| Sellick's Green *Som* | 2C **13** |
| Selworthy *Som* | 2B **6** |
| Sennen *Corn* | 3A **30** |
| Sennen Cove *Corn* | 3A **30** |
| Seven Ash *Som* | 3D **7** |
| Seworgan *Corn* | 1B **32** |
| Shaldon *Devn* | 3D **19** |
| Shallowford *Devn* | 2D **5** |
| Shaugh Prior *Devn* | 1B **26** |
| Shebbear *Devn* | 3D **9** |
| Sheepstor *Devn* | 1B **26** |
| Sheepwash *Devn* | 3D **9** |
| Sheldon *Devn* | 3B **12** |
| Sherford *Devn* | 2D **29** |
| Sherwood Green *Devn* | 1E **9** |
| Sheviock *Corn* | 2D **25** |
| Shillingford *Devn* | 1D **11** |
| Shillingford St George *Devn* | 2D **19** |
| Shinner's Bridge *Devn* | 1D **27** |
| Shiphay *Torb* | 1A **28** |
| Shirwell *Devn* | 3B **4** |
| Shobrooke *Devn* | 3C **11** |
| Shop *Devn* | 2C **8** |

| | |
|---|---|
| Shop *Corn* | 2B **8** |
| (nr Bude) | |
| Shop *Corn* | 3A **14** |
| (nr Padstow) | |
| Shoreditch *Som* | 1C **13** |
| Shortacombe *Devn* | 2D **17** |
| Shortlanesend *Corn* | 3C **23** |
| Shorton *Torb* | 1A **28** |
| Shute *Devn* | 1C **21** |
| (nr Axminster) | |
| Shute *Devn* | 3C **11** |
| (nr Crediton) | |
| Sid *Devn* | 2B **20** |
| Sidbury *Devn* | 1B **20** |
| Sidford *Devn* | 1B **20** |
| Sidmouth *Devn* | 2B **20** |
| Sigford *Devn* | 3B **18** |
| Silverton *Devn* | 3D **11** |
| Simonsbath *Som* | 3D **5** |
| Sithney *Corn* | 3D **31** |
| Skilgate *Som* | 1D **11** |
| Sladesbridge *Corn* | 3C **15** |
| Slapton *Devn* | 3A **28** |
| Slaughterbridge *Corn* | 2D **15** |
| Sloncombe *Devn* | 2B **18** |
| Slough Green *Som* | 1C **13** |
| Smallbrook *Devn* | 1C **19** |
| Smallridge *Devn* | 3D **13** |
| Smeatharpe *Devn* | 2C **13** |
| Smithincott *Devn* | 2A **12** |
| Snapper *Devn* | 3B **4** |
| Soldon Cross *Devn* | 2C **8** |
| Sourton *Devn* | 1D **17** |
| South Allington *Devn* | 3D **29** |
| South Brent *Devn* | 2C **27** |
| South Chard *Som* | 3D **13** |
| South Common *Devn* | 3D **13** |
| Southcott *Devn* | 2D **9** |
| (nr Great Torrington) | |
| Southcott *Devn* | 1D **17** |
| (nr Okehampton) | |
| Southerly *Devn* | 2D **17** |
| Southerton *Devn* | 1A **20** |
| South Hill *Corn* | 3B **16** |
| South Hole *Devn* | 1B **8** |
| South Huish *Devn* | 2C **29** |
| South Knighton *Devn* | 3C **19** |
| Southleigh *Devn* | 1C **21** |
| South Milton *Devn* | 2D **29** |
| South Molton *Devn* | 1B **10** |
| South Petherwin *Corn* | 2B **16** |
| South Pool *Devn* | 2D **29** |
| South Radworthy *Devn* | 3D **5** |
| South Tawton *Devn* | 1A **18** |
| South Town *Devn* | 2D **19** |
| South Wheatley *Corn* | 1A **16** |
| South Zeal *Devn* | 1A **18** |
| Sowton *Devn* | 1D **19** |
| Sparkwell *Devn* | 2B **26** |
| Splatt *Corn* | 2A **16** |
| Spreyton *Devn* | 1B **18** |
| Staddiscombe *Plym* | 2B **26** |
| Staddon *Devn* | 3C **8** |
| Stag's Head *Devn* | 1A **10** |
| Staple Cross *Devn* | 1A **12** |
| Staple Fitzpaine *Som* | 2C **13** |
| Staplegrove *Som* | 1C **13** |

| | |
|---|---|
| Staplehay *Som* | 1C **13** |
| Stapley *Som* | 2B **12** |
| Starcross *Devn* | 2D **19** |
| Start *Devn* | 3A **28** |
| Stathe *Som* | 1D **13** |
| Staverton *Devn* | 1D **27** |
| Stawley *Som* | 1A **12** |
| Stenalees *Corn* | 2A **24** |
| Stenhill *Devn* | 2A **12** |
| Stevenstone *Devn* | 2E **9** |
| Stewley *Som* | 2D **13** |
| Stibb *Corn* | 2B **8** |
| Stibb Cross *Devn* | 2D **9** |
| Sticker *Corn* | 2D **23** |
| Sticklepath *Devn* | 1A **18** |
| Stithians *Corn* | 1B **32** |
| Stockland *Devn* | 3C **13** |
| Stockleigh English *Devn* | 3C **11** |
| Stockleigh Pomeroy *Devn* | 3C **11** |
| Stocklinch *Som* | 2D **13** |
| Stogumber *Som* | 3C **7** |
| Stoke *Devn* | 1B **8** |
| Stoke Canon *Devn* | 1D **19** |
| Stoke Climsland *Corn* | 3B **16** |
| Stoke Fleming *Devn* | 3A **28** |
| Stoke Gabriel *Devn* | 2A **28** |
| Stokeinteignhead *Devn* | 3D **19** |
| Stokenham *Devn* | 3A **28** |
| Stoke Pero *Som* | 2A **6** |
| Stoke Rivers *Devn* | 3C **5** |
| Stoke St Gregory *Som* | 1D **13** |
| Stoke St Mary *Som* | 1C **13** |
| Stoneyford *Devn* | 3A **12** |
| Stony Cross *Devn* | 1E **9** |
| Stoodleigh *Devn* | 3C **5** |
| (nr Barnstaple) | |
| Stoodleigh *Devn* | 2D **11** |
| (nr Tiverton) | |
| Stoptide *Corn* | 3B **14** |
| Stowford *Devn* | 2A **20** |
| (nr Colaton Raleigh) | |
| Stowford *Devn* | 2C **5** |
| (nr Combe Martin) | |
| Stowford *Devn* | 2C **17** |
| (nr Tavistock) | |
| Stratton *Corn* | 3B **8** |
| Stream *Som* | 3C **7** |
| Street *Som* | 3D **13** |
| (nr Chard) | |
| Street *Corn* | 1A **16** |
| Street Ash *Som* | 2C **13** |
| Strete *Devn* | 3A **28** |
| Stringston *Som* | 2D **7** |
| Summercourt *Corn* | 2C **23** |
| Sutcombe *Devn* | 2C **8** |
| Sweetham *Devn* | 1C **19** |
| Sweets *Corn* | 1D **15** |
| Sweetshouse *Corn* | 1A **24** |
| Swell *Som* | 1D **13** |
| Swimbridge *Devn* | 1A **10** |
| Swimbridge Newland *Devn* | 3C **5** |
| Sydenham Damerel *Devn* | 3C **17** |

**T**

| | |
|---|---|
| Taddiport *Devn* | 2D **9** |
| Talaton *Devn* | 1A **20** |

| | |
|---|---|
| Taleford *Devn* | 1A **20** |
| Talskiddy *Corn* | 1D **23** |
| Tamerton Foliot *Plym* | 1A **26** |
| Tarr *Som* | 3D **7** |
| Tatworth *Som* | 3D **13** |
| **Taunton** *Som* | **35** (1C **13**) |
| **Tavistock** *Devn* | 3C **17** |
| Taw Green *Devn* | 1A **18** |
| Tawstock *Devn* | 1E **9** |
| Tedburn St Mary *Devn* | 1C **19** |
| Teigncombe *Devn* | 2A **18** |
| Teigngrace *Devn* | 3C **19** |
| Teignmouth *Devn* | 3D **19** |
| Temple *Corn* | 3D **15** |
| Templeton *Devn* | 2C **11** |
| Terhill *Som* | 3D **7** |
| Tetcott *Devn* | 1B **16** |
| Thelbridge *Devn* | 2B **10** |
| Thornbury *Devn* | 3D **9** |
| Thorncombe *Dors* | 3D **13** |
| Thorndon Cross *Devn* | 1D **17** |
| Thorne St Margaret *Som* | 1A **12** |
| Thornfalcon *Som* | 1C **13** |
| Thornhillhead *Devn* | 2D **9** |
| Thorverton *Devn* | 3D **11** |
| Three Burrows *Corn* | 3B **22** |
| Threemilestone *Corn* | 3B **22** |
| Throwleigh *Devn* | 1A **18** |
| Thrushelton *Devn* | 2C **17** |
| Thurdon *Corn* | 2B **8** |
| Thurlbear *Som* | 1C **13** |
| Thurlestone *Devn* | 2C **29** |
| Tideford *Corn* | 2D **25** |
| Tideford Cross *Corn* | 1D **25** |
| Tigley *Devn* | 1D **27** |
| Timberscombe *Som* | 2B **6** |
| Tinhay *Devn* | 2B **16** |
| Tintagel *Corn* | 2C **15** |
| Tippacott *Devn* | 2D **5** |
| Tipton St John *Devn* | 1A **20** |
| Titchberry *Devn* | 1B **8** |
| Titson *Corn* | 3B **8** |
| **Tiverton** *Devn* | 2D **11** |
| Tivington *Som* | 2B **6** |
| Tolland *Som* | 3D **7** |
| Tonedale *Som* | 1B **12** |
| Topsham *Devn* | 2D **19** |
| **Torbay** *Torb* | 1B **28** |
| Torbryan *Devn* | 1A **28** |
| Torcross *Devn* | 3A **28** |
| Torpoint *Corn* | 2A **26** |
| **Torquay** *Torb* | 1B **28** |
| Torr *Devn* | 2B **26** |
| Torre *Som* | 3C **7** |
| Torre *Torb* | 1B **28** |
| Totnes *Devn* | 1A **28** |
| Towans, The *Corn* | 2C **31** |
| Towednack *Corn* | 2B **30** |
| Townshend *Corn* | 2C **31** |
| Traboe *Corn* | 2B **32** |
| Treator *Corn* | 3B **14** |
| Trebarber *Corn* | 1C **23** |
| Trebartha *Corn* | 3A **16** |
| Trebarwith *Corn* | 2C **15** |
| Trebetherick *Corn* | 3B **14** |
| Treborough *Som* | 3C **7** |
| Trebudannon *Corn* | 1C **23** |
| Trebullett *Corn* | 3B **16** |
| Treburley *Corn* | 3B **16** |
| Treburrick *Corn* | 3A **14** |
| Trebyan *Corn* | 1A **24** |
| Trecott *Devn* | 3A **10** |
| Tredaule *Corn* | 2A **16** |
| Tredavoe *Corn* | 3B **30** |
| Tredinnick *Corn* | 1B **24** |
| | (nr Bodmin) |
| Tredinnick *Corn* | 2C **25** |
| | (nr Looe) |
| Tredinnick *Corn* | 3B **14** |
| | (nr Padstow) |
| Treen *Corn* | 3A **30** |
| | (nr Land's End) |
| Treen *Corn* | 2B **30** |
| | (nr St Ives) |
| Trefrew *Corn* | 2D **15** |
| Tregada *Corn* | 2B **16** |
| Tregadillett *Corn* | 2A **16** |
| Tregarne *Corn* | 2B **32** |
| Tregear *Corn* | 2C **23** |
| Tregeare *Corn* | 2A **16** |
| Tregeseal *Corn* | 2A **30** |
| Tregiskey *Corn* | 3A **24** |
| Tregole *Corn* | 1D **15** |
| Tregonetha *Corn* | 1D **23** |
| Tregonhawke *Corn* | 2A **26** |
| Tregony *Corn* | 3D **23** |
| Tregoodwell *Corn* | 2D **15** |
| Tregorrick *Corn* | 2A **24** |
| Tregoss *Corn* | 1D **23** |
| Tregowris *Corn* | 2B **32** |
| Tregrehan Mills *Corn* | 2A **24** |
| Tregullon *Corn* | 1A **24** |
| Tregurrian *Corn* | 1C **23** |
| Trehan *Corn* | 2A **26** |
| Trehunist *Corn* | 1D **25** |
| Trekenner *Corn* | 3B **16** |
| Trekenning *Corn* | 1D **23** |
| Treknow *Corn* | 2C **15** |
| Trelan *Corn* | 3B **32** |
| Trelash *Corn* | 1D **15** |
| Trelassick *Corn* | 2C **23** |
| Treligga *Corn* | 2C **15** |
| Trelights *Corn* | 3B **14** |
| Trelill *Corn* | 3C **15** |
| Trelissick *Corn* | 1C **32** |
| Tremail *Corn* | 2D **15** |
| Tremaine *Corn* | 2A **16** |
| Tremar *Corn* | 1C **25** |
| Trematon *Corn* | 2D **25** |
| Tremore *Corn* | 1A **24** |
| Trenance *Corn* | 1C **23** |
| | (nr Newquay) |
| Trenance *Corn* | 3B **14** |
| | (nr Padstow) |
| Trenarren *Corn* | 3A **24** |
| Trencreek *Corn* | 1C **23** |
| Trendeal *Corn* | 2C **23** |
| Trenear *Corn* | 2D **31** |
| Treneglos *Corn* | 2A **16** |
| Trenewan *Corn* | 2B **24** |
| Trengune *Corn* | 1D **15** |
| Trentishoe *Devn* | 2C **5** |
| Trerulefoot *Corn* | 2D **25** |
| Trescowe *Corn* | 2C **31** |
| Tresillian *Corn* | 3C **23** |
| Tresinney *Corn* | 2D **15** |
| Treskillard *Corn* | 2D **31** |
| Treskinnick Cross *Corn* | 1A **16** |
| Tresmeer *Corn* | 2A **16** |
| Tresparrett *Corn* | 1D **15** |
| Tresparrett Posts *Corn* | 1D **15** |
| Treswithian *Corn* | 2D **31** |
| Trethosa *Corn* | 2D **23** |
| Trethurgy *Corn* | 2A **24** |
| Trevadlock *Corn* | 3A **16** |
| Trevalga *Corn* | 2C **15** |
| Trevance *Corn* | 3B **14** |
| Trevanger *Corn* | 3B **14** |
| Trevanson *Corn* | 3B **14** |
| Trevarrack *Corn* | 2B **30** |
| Trevarren *Corn* | 1D **23** |
| Trevarrian *Corn* | 1C **23** |
| Trevarrick *Corn* | 3D **23** |
| Treveighan *Corn* | 3C **15** |
| Trevellas *Corn* | 2B **22** |
| Trevelmond *Corn* | 1C **25** |
| Treverva *Corn* | 1B **32** |
| Trevescan *Corn* | 3A **30** |
| Trevia *Corn* | 2C **15** |
| Trevigro *Corn* | 1D **25** |
| Trevilley *Corn* | 3A **30** |
| Treviscoe *Corn* | 2D **23** |
| Trevivian *Corn* | 2D **15** |
| Trevone *Corn* | 3A **14** |
| Trew *Corn* | 3D **31** |
| Trewalder *Corn* | 2C **15** |
| Trewarlett *Corn* | 2B **16** |
| Trewarmett *Corn* | 2C **15** |
| Trewassa *Corn* | 2D **15** |
| Treween *Corn* | 2A **16** |
| Trewellard *Corn* | 2A **30** |
| Trewen *Corn* | 2A **16** |
| Trewennack *Corn* | 3D **31** |
| Trewetha *Corn* | 3C **15** |
| Trewidland *Corn* | 2C **25** |
| Trewint *Corn* | 1D **15** |
| Trewithian *Corn* | 1C **32** |
| Trewoofe *Corn* | 3B **30** |
| Trewoon *Corn* | 2D **23** |
| Treworthal *Corn* | 1C **32** |
| Treyarnon *Corn* | 3A **14** |
| Trimstone *Devn* | 2B **4** |
| Triscombe *Som* | 3D **7** |
| Trispen *Corn* | 2C **23** |
| Troon *Corn* | 2D **31** |
| Trull *Som* | 1C **13** |
| **Truro** *Corn* | 3C **23** |
| Trusham *Devn* | 2C **19** |
| Tuckenhay *Devn* | 2A **28** |
| Tuckingmill *Corn* | 3A **22** |
| Turfmoor *Devn* | 3C **13** |
| Turnchapel *Plym* | 2A **26** |
| Tutwell *Corn* | 3B **16** |
| Twelveheads *Corn* | 3B **22** |
| Twitchen *Devn* | 3D **5** |
| Two Bridges *Devn* | 3A **18** |
| Two Mile Oak *Devn* | 1A **28** |
| Tythecott *Devn* | 2D **9** |
| Tytherleigh *Devn* | 3D **13** |
| Tywardreath *Corn* | 2A **24** |
| Tywardreath Highway *Corn* | 2A **24** |

## U

Uffculme *Devn* ............................ 2A **12**
Ugborough *Devn* ......................... 2C **27**
Umberleigh *Devn* ........................ 1A **10**
Underwood *Plym* ......................... 2B **26**
Upcott *Devn* ................................. 3E **9**
Up Exe *Devn* ............................... 3D **11**
Upham *Devn* ................................ 3C **11**
Uplowman *Devn* ......................... 2A **12**
Uplyme *Devn* ............................... 1D **21**
Upottery *Devn* ............................. 3C **13**
Upper Cheddon *Som* ................... 1C **13**
Uppincott *Devn* ........................... 3C **11**
Upton *Corn* .................................. 3B **8**
..................................... (nr Bude)
Upton *Corn* .................................. 3A **16**
.................................. (nr Liskeard)
Upton *Devn* ................................. 3A **12**
................................... (nr Honiton)
Upton *Devn* ................................. 2D **29**
............................... (nr Kingsbridge)
Upton *Som* .................................. 1D **11**
Upton Cross *Corn* ....................... 3A **16**
Upton Hellions *Devn* ................... 3C **11**
Upton Pyne *Devn* ........................ 1D **19**
Uton *Devn* ................................... 1C **19**

## V

Valley Truckle *Corn* ..................... 2D **15**
Yellow *Som* .................................. 3C **7**
Velly *Devn* ................................... 1B **8**
Venhay *Devn* ............................... 2B **10**
Venn *Devn* ................................... 2D **29**
Venngreen *Devn* ......................... 2C **8**
Venn Ottery *Devn* ....................... 1A **20**
Venny Tedburn *Devn* ................... 1C **19**
Venterdon *Corn* ........................... 3B **16**
Veryan *Corn* ................................ 1D **33**
Veryan Green *Corn* ..................... 1D **33**
Vicarage *Devn* ............................ 2C **21**
Victoria *Corn* ............................... 1D **23**
Virginstow *Devn* .......................... 1B **16**

## W

Wadbrook *Devn* ........................... 3D **13**
Waddeton *Devn* ........................... 2A **28**
Waddon *Devn* .............................. 3C **19**
Wadebridge *Corn* ........................ 3B **14**
Wadeford *Som* ............................ 2D **13**
Wainhouse Corner *Corn* .............. 1D **15**
Walkhampton *Devn* ..................... 1B **26**
Wall *Corn* .................................... 2D **31**
Wambrook *Som* ........................... 3C **13**
Warbstow *Corn* ........................... 1A **16**
Warfleet *Devn* ............................. 2A **28**
Warkleigh *Devn* ........................... 1A **10**
Warleggan *Corn* .......................... 1B **24**
Washaway *Corn* .......................... 1A **24**
Washbourne *Devn* ....................... 2D **27**
Washfield *Devn* ........................... 2D **11**
Washford *Som* ............................. 2C **7**
Washford Pyne *Devn* ................... 2C **11**
Watchet *Som* ............................... 2C **7**
Watcombe *Torb* ........................... 1B **28**

Water *Devn* ................................. 2B **18**
Waterloo *Corn* ............................. 3D **15**
Waterrow *Som* ............................. 1A **12**
Way Village *Devn* ........................ 2C **11**
Weare Giffard *Devn* ..................... 1D **9**
Week *Devn* .................................. 1E **9**
.................................. (nr Barnstaple)
Week *Devn* .................................. 3A **10**
.................................. (nr Okehampton)
Week *Devn* .................................. 2B **10**
................................ (nr South Molton)
Week *Devn* .................................. 1D **27**
..................................... (nr Totnes)
Week *Som* ................................... 3B **6**
Weeke *Devn* ................................ 3B **10**
Week Green *Corn* ........................ 1A **16**
Week St Mary *Corn* ..................... 1A **16**
Welcombe *Devn* .......................... 2B **8**
**Wellington** *Som* ....................... 1B **12**
Wellswood *Torb* ........................... 1B **28**
Welsford *Devn* ............................. 1B **8**
Wembury *Devn* ............................ 3B **26**
Wembworthy *Devn* ...................... 3A **10**
Wendron *Corn* ............................. 2D **31**
Wenfordbridge *Corn* .................... 3C **15**
Werrington *Corn* .......................... 2B **16**
West Alvington *Devn* ................... 2D **29**
West Anstey *Devn* ....................... 1C **11**
West Bagborough *Som* ................ 3D **7**
West Buckland *Devn* .................... 3C **5**
.................................. (nr Barnstaple)
West Buckland *Devn* .................... 2C **29**
................................ (nr Thurlestone)
West Buckland *Som* ..................... 1B **12**
West Charleton *Devn* ................... 2D **29**
Westcott *Devn* ............................. 3A **12**
West Curry *Corn* .......................... 1A **16**
West Down *Devn* ......................... 2B **4**
Westdowns *Corn* ......................... 2C **15**
Westford *Som* .............................. 1B **12**
West Hatch *Som* .......................... 1C **13**
West Hill *Devn* ............................. 1A **20**
Westlake *Devn* ............................ 2C **27**
West Leigh *Devn* ......................... 3A **10**
Westleigh *Devn* ........................... 1D **9**
.................................... (nr Bideford)
Westleigh *Devn* ........................... 2A **12**
.................................... (nr Tiverton)
West Looe *Corn* .......................... 2C **25**
West Lyng *Som* ........................... 1D **13**
West Monkton *Som* ..................... 1C **13**
West Newton *Som* ....................... 1C **13**
West Ogwell *Devn* ....................... 1A **28**
Weston *Devn* ............................... 3B **12**
.................................... (nr Honiton)
Weston *Devn* ............................... 2B **20**
................................... (nr Sidmouth)
West Panson *Devn* ...................... 1B **16**
West Pentire *Corn* ....................... 1B **22**
West Porlock *Som* ....................... 2A **6**
Westport *Som* .............................. 2D **13**
West Putford *Devn* ...................... 2C **8**
West Quantoxhead *Som* .............. 2D **7**
West Sandford *Devn* .................... 3C **11**
West Taphouse *Corn* ................... 1B **24**
Westward Ho! *Devn* .................... 1D **9**
Westwood *Devn* .......................... 1A **20**

West Worlington *Devn* ................. 2B **10**
West Youlstone *Corn* ................... 2B **8**
Weycroft *Devn* ............................ 1D **21**
Whatley *Som* ............................... 3D **13**
Wheatley *Devn* ............................ 1C **19**
Wheddon Cross *Som* ................... 3B **6**
Whiddon *Devn* ............................. 3D **9**
Whiddon Down *Devn* ................... 1A **18**
Whimble *Devn* ............................. 3C **8**
Whimple *Devn* ............................. 1A **20**
Whipton *Devn* .............................. 1D **19**
Whitchurch *Devn* ......................... 3C **17**
Whitchurch Canonicorum *Dors* ......... 1D **21**
White Cross *Corn* ........................ 3D **31**
Whitecross *Corn* .......................... 3B **14**
Whitefield *Som* ............................ 1A **12**
Whitehall *Devn* ............................ 2B **12**
Whitelackington *Som* ................... 2D **13**
Whitemoor *Corn* .......................... 2D **23**
Whitestaunton *Som* ..................... 2C **13**
Whitestone *Devn* ......................... 1C **19**
Whiteworks *Devn* ........................ 3A **18**
Whitford *Devn* ............................. 1C **21**
Whitleigh *Plym* ............................ 2A **26**
Whitnage *Devn* ............................ 2A **12**
Whitstone *Corn* ........................... 1A **16**
Wick *Devn* ................................... 3B **12**
Widecombe in the Moor *Devn* .......... 3B **18**
Widegates *Corn* .......................... 2C **25**
Widemouth Bay *Corn* ................... 3B **8**
Widworthy *Devn* .......................... 1C **21**
Wiggaton *Devn* ........................... 1B **20**
Wilcove *Corn* ............................... 2A **26**
Willand *Devn* ............................... 2A **12**
Willett *Som* .................................. 3D **7**
Williton *Som* ................................ 2C **7**
Wilmington *Devn* ......................... 1C **21**
Windmill Hill *Som* ........................ 2D **13**
Winkleigh *Devn* ........................... 3A **10**
Winnard's Perch *Corn* ................. 1D **23**
Winsford *Som* .............................. 3B **6**
Winsham *Devn* ............................ 3A **4**
Winsham *Som* .............................. 3D **13**
Winswell *Devn* ............................ 2D **9**
Winterhay Green *Som* .................. 2D **13**
Witheridge *Devn* .......................... 2C **11**
Withiel *Corn* ................................ 1D **23**
Withiel Florey *Som* ...................... 3B **6**
Withleigh *Devn* ............................ 2D **11**
Withycombe *Som* ......................... 2C **7**
Withycombe Raleigh *Devn* ........... 2A **20**
Withypool *Som* ............................ 3A **6**
Wiveliscombe *Som* ...................... 1A **12**
Wolborough *Devn* ....................... 3C **19**
Wonson *Devn* .............................. 2A **18**
Woodacott *Devn* ......................... 3C **8**
Woodbridge *Devn* ....................... 1B **20**
Woodbury *Devn* ........................... 2A **20**
Woodbury Salterton *Devn* ............ 2A **20**
Woodcombe *Som* ........................ 2B **6**
Woodford *Corn* ........................... 2B **8**
Woodford *Devn* ........................... 2D **27**
Woodford *Plym* ........................... 2B **26**
Woodhill *Som* .............................. 1D **13**
Woodhuish *Devn* ......................... 2B **28**
Woodland *Devn* ........................... 1D **27**
Woodland Head *Devn* .................. 1B **18**

Woodleigh *Devn*.................................2D **29**
Woodmanton *Devn*............................2A **20**
Woodtown *Devn*.................................1D **9**
.............................................(nr Bideford)
Woodtown *Devn*.................................1D **9**
............................................(nr Littleham)
Woody Bay *Devn*...............................2C **5**
Woolacombe *Devn*............................2A **4**
Woolcotts *Som*.................................3B **6**
Woolfardisworthy *Devn*......................1C **8**
.............................................(nr Bideford)
Woolfardisworthy *Devn*.....................3C **11**
..............................................(nr Crediton)
Woolley *Corn*......................................2B **8**
Woolsery *Devn*..................................1C **8**
Woolston *Devn*.................................2D **29**

Woolston Green *Devn*.........................1D **27**
Woolwell *Devn*..................................1B **26**
Wootton Courtenay *Som* ...................2B **6**
Wootton Fitzpaine *Dors*....................1D **21**
Wotter *Devn*......................................1B **26**
Wrafton *Devn*......................................3A **4**
Wrangway *Som*................................2B **12**
Wrantage *Som*.................................1D **13**
Wreyland *Devn*.................................2B **18**
Wyke *Devn*.......................................1C **19**

## Y

Yarcombe *Devn*................................3C **13**
Yarde *Som*...........................................3C **7**
Yarnscombe *Devn*.............................1E **9**

Yawl *Devn*.........................................1D **21**
Yealmpton *Devn*..............................2B **26**
Yelland *Devn*.......................................3A **4**
Yelverton *Devn*................................1B **26**
Yeoford *Devn*...................................1B **18**
Yeolmbridge *Corn* ...........................2B **16**
Yeo Mill *Devn*...................................1C **11**
Yettington *Devn* ..............................2A **20**

## Z

Zeal Monachorum *Devn*...................3B **10**
Zelah *Corn*.......................................2C **23**
Zennor *Corn*.....................................2B **30**

Published by Geographers' A-Z Map Company Limited
An imprint of HarperCollins Publishers
Westerhill Road
Bishopbriggs
Glasgow
G64 2QT

www.az.co.uk
a-z.maps@harpercollins.co.uk

HarperCollinsPublishers, Macken House, 39/40 Mayor Street Upper, Dublin 1, D01 C9W8, Ireland

1st edition 2023

© Collins Bartholomew Ltd 2023

This product uses map data licenced from Ordnance Survey
© Crown copyright and database rights 2022 OS AC0000808974

AZ, A-Z and AtoZ are registered trademarks of Geographers' A-Z Map Company Limited

A catalogue record for this book is available from the British Library.

ISBN 978-0-00-856057-7

10 9 8 7 6 5 4 3 2 1

Printed in India